The UAW

This book analyzes the multi-faceted scandal that has tarnished the reputation of the United Auto Workers (UAW), an iconic union revered for its commitment to union democracy and ethical practices, showing what went wrong to lead the spread of corruption and how to remedy it.

Masters and Goeddeke provide a historical context of the rise and decline of the UAW, leading to "a culture of corruption" and resulting in the indictment or conviction of 15 union and corporate officials for the misuse of tens of millions of dollars. The book evaluates the various proposed reforms of the UAW's financial practices and ethical standards, including the possibility of a government takeover. It raises questions about the wisdom of such a takeover, based on the problems associated with the government takeover of the Teamsters. The authors recommend that the UAW convene a special constitutional convention to consider reforms in governance and hiring practices.

Providing a clear depiction of this scandal and the UAW's systemic flaws, and suggesting potential remedies, this book will appeal to the tens of thousands of union officers and members keenly interested in the state of labor and an iconic union, their corporate counterparts in management, academics, students, and journalists in the fields of business and society, employee relations, law, labor relations, and management.

Frank Goeddeke, Jr. is a Senior Lecturer in the Mike Ilitch School of Business at Wayne State University in Detroit, MI. He is a retired automaker and has held elected and staff positions in the UAW and AFT. He holds a PhD in Management from the University of Florida, an MBA from Rollins College, and a MAS and BS from Embry-Riddle Aeronautical University. He has taught for over 20 years at several higher education institutions. He has been published in several journals, including *Journal of Organizational Behavior* and *Organizational Research Methods*. Additionally, he is a former US Peace Corps Volunteer in Mongolia.

Marick F. Masters is a Professor of Management in the Mike Ilitch School of Business at Wayne State University, Detroit, Michigan, USA.

The UAW

An Iconic Union Falls into Scandal

Frank Goeddeke, Jr. and Marick F. Masters

Routledge
Taylor & Francis Group

NEW YORK AND LONDON

First published 2021
by Routledge
52 Vanderbilt Avenue, New York, NY 10017

and by Routledge
2 Park Square, Milton Park, Abingdon, Oxon OX14 4RN

Routledge is an imprint of the Taylor & Francis Group, an informa business

Library of Congress Cataloging-in-Publication Data
Names: Goeddeke, Frank, Jr., author. | Masters, Marick Francis,
1954- author.
Title: The UAW : an iconic union falls into scandal / Frank Goeddeke Jr. and
Marick F. Masters.
Description: New York, NY : Routledge, 2021. | Includes bibliographical
references and index.
Identifiers: LCCN 2020043761 (print) | LCCN 2020043762 (ebook) |
ISBN 9780367629625 (hbk) | ISBN 9780367622732 (pbk) |
ISBN 9781003111610 (ebk)
Subjects: LCSH: International Union, United Automobile, Aircraft, and
Agricultural Implement Workers of America--History. |
Labor unions--Corrupt practices--United States--History.
Classification: LCC HD6515.A82 .I57365 2021 (print) |
LCC HD6515.A82 (ebook) | DDC 331.88/1292220973--dc23
LC record available at https://lccn.loc.gov/2020043761
LC ebook record available at https://lccn.loc.gov/2020043762

ISBN: 978-0-367-62962-5 (hbk)
ISBN: 978-0-367-62273-2 (pbk)
ISBN: 978-1-003-11161-0 (ebk)

Typeset in Sabon
by Taylor & Francis Books

Contents

Figures

Tables

Boxes

Preface

We made the decision to write this book in late 2019 as the United Auto Workers (UAW) was buffeted by revelations of scandal involving officials at its highest levels, with the associated involvement of selected corporate officials at Fiat Chrysler Auto (FCA, formerly Chrysler). The revelations had forced the resignation of the sitting International President of the UAW in November 2019, leading to a grass-roots movement to call a special constitutional convention to require the direct election of the union's international officers among others. While the UAW had long been known as a one-party organization, run by the Administrative Caucus founded under Walter Reuther, it had also enjoyed a reputation for being relatively democratic among unions and free of corruption. The torrent of reported misconduct involving the illegal use of large amounts of union-connected money shocked us and other friends of the iconic union.

We bring combined experience from the academia and practice when it comes to the UAW and labor-management relations. Both of us currently serve on the faculty of the Department of Management and Information Systems of the Mike Ilitch School of Business at Wayne State University (WSU). Each of our careers intersects with the UAW. Frank Goeddeke is a retired auto worker who has been a UAW member since 1979. He has held elected positions in his UAW and former NEA/AFT locals. He also worked for a time on the organizing staff of the International UAW at Solidarity House, the union's national headquarters located in Detroit. Marick Masters served as director of Labor@Wayne at WSU for nearly 11 years, which included the Douglas A. Fraser Center for Workplace Issues, the namesake being a former UAW International President. He worked with various officials and staff of the UAW and the Detroit 3 auto companies (FCA, Ford, and General Motors) on academic-related projects associated with the education of union members and the study of labor-management relations. [In the interest of full disclosure, Labor@Wayne received contributions made by the UAW-Detroit 3 national training centers to the Fraser Center through WSU to support labor education.]

Both of us believe strongly that labor unions play a legitimate role in the workplace and society. We recognize the great contributions the UAW has made to improve the working lives of auto workers and build a stronger middle class in the nation. The overwhelming majority of staff and officials of the UAW serve the membership honorably and well. The rank-and-file of the UAW are dedicated to producing high-quality products and services.

We approach this book from the perspective of understanding the scandal in the hope that this knowledge can help to make the UAW a better institution. Our desire is for a stronger UAW, not just in terms of its adherence to the highest standards of ethical conduct but also its capacity to represent members in its dealings with employers and in the realm of politics as well. What can we learn from the genesis, nature, and scope of the scandal? What actions should be taken to prevent recurrence of such overt acts of wrongdoing? Is a government takeover of the UAW warranted?

We address these and other related questions from an analysis of the data on what happened at the UAW and what knowledge we can draw from experience on how other union scandals have been handled, particularly with respect to the federal government's takeover of the International Brotherhood of Teamsters (IBT, Teamsters) in the late 1980s. Our analysis focuses on more than the details of the demonstrable wrongdoing. It puts the events into the broader organizational and industrial context within which the UAW has operated. A strong interaction exists between the administration and governance of the UAW, the unions' relationships with the Detroit 3 in bargaining contracts, and the state of the auto industry. We cannot fully appreciate the scandal in isolation. The overt acts of criminality occurred in the context of collective bargaining relationships between the UAW and the Detroit 3, which faced severe financial challenges requiring massive restructuring of the companies. In the midst of this restructuring, the UAW itself faced internal financial problems correlated with the down-turn in the fortunes of the domestic auto manufacturing industry, leading to huge job losses.

We gathered data from several sources to build a narrative about how the scandal evolved in different parts of the UAW and its joint training centers with the Detroit 3 (two of them in particular). Extensive background information was collected on history of the administration and governance of the UAW, the evolving state of the domestic auto manufacturing industry, collective bargaining agreements between the UAW and the Detroit 3 over the past several cycles, going back to before the Great Recession, and the history of joint training centers initiated by the UAW and Detroit 3 in the 1980s to address issues of competitiveness (or the lack thereof). Data on the companies' and the UAW's finances supplemented this background, along with the finances of the joint training centers and selected charities sponsored by UAW leaders that were implicated. We relied on news reports and civil and criminal complaints and pleadings for information on the misconduct investigated and prosecuted by the US Attorney's office. In addition, we reviewed the literature on union corruption in general and at the IBT in particular.

In researching this book, we did not conduct any formal interviews with anyone on either the management or union side. Nor did we interview anyone associated with investigating or prosecuting the cases of wrongdoing. We made no attempt to include proprietary data or information otherwise not publicly available. Based on our work histories, however, we did have a rich reservoir of knowledge to tap about the inner-workings of the UAW and collective bargaining relationships between the parties.

We want to emphasize that we are not writing this book about the individuals convicted or implicated in the wrongdoing. We make no judgment about individuals who have been implicated. Our analysis focuses on presenting information from news sources and the US Attorney's office on what happened in this case, recognizing that 15 high-ranking officials of the UAW and FCA (which has recently merged with PSA Groupe, agreeing to change the name of new entity to Stellantis in 2021) have been convicted.

As a preview, we believe that the UAW scandals, although a serious breach of trust of UAW members and the institution's legacy, involved relatively few people who were motivated by personal greed. It appears that high-ranking FCA executives had as a motivation tilting labor-management relations for the company's advantage. But the overwhelming majority of UAW officials and staff are highly ethical and committed to the union's mission. The UAW is not mob-infested as the IBT was. And democratic reforms *per se* are not perfect antidotes, though the merit consideration on how to position the union to become a more effective representative in the future.

List of Acronyms and Abbreviations

Administrative Caucus	The dominant caucus within the UAW, formerly known as the Reuther Caucus
AFL	American Federation of Labor
AFL-CIO	American Federation of Labor - Congress of Industrial Unions
AIF	Annual Improvement Factor
Alliance for Labor Action	Alternative to the AFL-CIO that lasted only a few years
Big 3	General Motors (GM), Ford, and Fiat Chrysler (FCA)
Black Lake	UAW Education Center in Onaway, Michigan
CAP	Community Action Program (UAW political action committee)
CBA	Collective bargaining agreements
CEO	Chief Executive Officer

CHR	UAW-GM Center for Human Resources (joint programs)
CIO	Congress of Industrial Unions
COLA	Cost of Living Allowance
CW-1, CW-2, etc	Cooperating witness 1, cooperating witness 2, etc.
Detroit 3	General Motors (GM), Ford, and Fiat Chrysler (FCA)
DOJ	US Department of Justice
DOL	US Department of Labor
FBI	US Federal Bureau of Investigation
FCA	Fiat Chrysler Automobiles, NV
GDP	Gross domestic product
GM	General Motors
Great Recession	Recession that began in 2007
IBB	Interest-based bargaining
IBT	International Brotherhood of Teamsters (union)
IEB	UAW International Executive Board
IR	International Representative
IRS	Internal Revenue Service
JFR	Joint fund reimbursements
Landrum-Griffin Act	Labor Management Reporting and Disclosure Act
LM-2	US Department of Labor annual financial disclosure form for unions ($\geq$ $250,000 in annual receipts)
LM-3	US Department of Labor annual financial disclosure form for unions (< $250,000 in annual receipts)
LM-4	US Department of Labor annual financial disclosure form for unions (< $10,000 in annual receipts)
LMRA	Labor Management Relations Act, also known as the Taft-Hartley Act
LMRDA	Labor Management Reporting and Disclosure Act
LTLOF	Leave The Lights On Foundation, a charity run by General Holiefield
MBI	Member-based income, a measure to determine relative capacity of a union to finance its activities from member dues
NAFTA	North American Free Trade Agreement
NLRA	National Labor Relations Act, also known as the Wagner Act
NPC	UAW-Ford National Program Center (joint programs)
NTC	UAW-Chrysler National Training Center (joint programs)
OLMS	US Department of Labor Office of Labor-Management Standards

OPEC	Organization of the Petroleum Exporting Countries
PAC	Political action committee
PATCO	Professional Air Traffic Controllers Organization (union, 1968–1981)
PRB	Public Review Board, the UAW's final appellate body, composed of outside professionals
PSA	PSA Groupe (European auto manufacturer)
Reuther Caucus	The dominant caucus within the UAW, now known as the Administrative Caucus
RICO	Racketeer Influenced and Corrupt Organizations Act
RPSH	Renaissance Palm Springs Hotel
RUM	Revolutionary Union Movement
S&P	Standard & Poor's stock index
Solidarity House	Headquarters building for the UAW; also refers to the national UAW organization
SUB	Supplemental Unemployment Benefits
SUV	Sport utility vehicle
Taft-Hartley Act	Labor Management Relations Act
TARP	Troubled Assets Relief Program
UAW	United Auto Workers (union); International Union, United Automobile, Aerospace, and Agricultural Implement Workers of America
UAW Official A	Federal prosecutor's reference to former UAW President Gary Jones
UAW Official B	Federal prosecutor's reference to former UAW President Dennis Williams
UAWD	Unite All Workers for Democracy, a recent UAW dissident caucus
VEBA	Voluntary Employee Benefits Association, sometimes used for employee benefits
VP	Vice President
VW	Volkswagen, European auto manufacturer
Wagner Act	National Labor Relations Act

Introduction

Throughout its history, the United Auto Workers has symbolized the better angels of the American labor movement.[1] It prided itself in maintaining high standards of conduct in its operations and among officialdom, keeping the salaries of its leaders to modest levels and fighting vigorously to improve the economic lot of everyday working people.[2] Many associate the UAW with building the middle class in America, bringing the American Dream into the reach of millions.[3] This stalwart of economic and social justice also stood at the forefront of the civil rights movement, financing many of Dr. Martin Luther King's marches.[4]

Ironically, the UAW's very success in uplifting the well-being of working people bred stern opposition and outright hostility, notwithstanding its reputation for being a corruption-free union, in contrast, for example, to the often maligned International Brotherhood of Teamsters.[5] The UAW, Big 3 (now Detroit 3: Ford, General Motors, GM, and FCA/Chrysler, which will merge with PSA in 2021, taking the name of Stellantis)[6] auto companies, and the city of Detroit symbolized American manufacturing superiority and middle-class prosperity for decades.

Yet, as the saying goes, every good thing comes to an end. First came foreign competition and a crushing blow to the companies' finances.[7] In the 1980s and thereafter, auto manufacturing experienced episodes of sweeping job losses, which cratered the prosperity of Detroit and signified the falling competitiveness of American industry.[8] In the process, the UAW's status in society shrank vastly.[9] Between 1979 and 2008, the union's total membership dropped by more than one million.[10] The economically devastating impact of the Great Recession (2007–2009) on the cyclically vulnerable auto industry, coupled with the companies' unsustainable cost structures ridden with massive liabilities, led two of the Detroit 3—General Motors and Chrysler—into bankruptcy, while Ford Motor had earlier leveraged itself wholesale to avoid a similar fate.[11]

With the Detroit 3 in dire financial straits, staring at liquidation, the federal government rescued GM and Chrysler, infusing huge sums of money to the cash-strapped and then credit-unworthy companies.[12] Through herculean if not heroic efforts, the companies worked with the UAW to reverse the downturn and return them to profitability with remarkable swiftness.[13] They had partnered with the UAW to find a pathway to survival and renewed profitability, but not without having to inflict economic pain on thousands of workers and scores of communities who watched their manufacturing lifeblood collapse.[14] By 2015 and 2019, when the companies entered contract negotiations with the UAW, they faced rising demands to claim workers' fair share of the profits brought about in part through their sacrifices at the altar of competitiveness.

Indeed, the Detroit 3 had begun adding new workers to rebuild for the future.[15] Ford, for example, had increased its hourly workforce from the recession nadir of less than 35,000 in 2010 to more than 55,000 in 2019. While labor in auto will never likely see its ranks rise to the heights of the late 1970s, it has bounced back, and the UAW's membership has risen from a low of just above 355,000 in 2010 to more than 430,000 in 2018.[16]

Yet, whatever cause there may have been for celebration among the UAW leadership and rank-and-file fell apart in July 2017 as the first news reports of scandalous conduct appeared.[17] A steady drumbeat of revelations of illicit activity has since exposed deep and wide illegality, involving the embezzlement of millions of dollars for personal gain. As it enters the third decade of the twenty-first century, the UAW has a reputation in tatters, with the prospect of a government takeover looming.

At the time of this writing, the aggressive investigation led by the US Attorney's office had resulted in the indictment and conviction of 15 UAW and corporate officials, uncovered widespread misuse of company-provided funds earmarked for the two of the Detroit 3 companies' national training centers set up in the mid-1980s to promote productivity and quality, revealed the illegal or inappropriate use of union treasury monies for personal gain, and raised questions about whether the training centers had compromised the institutional integrity of the once iconic union beyond reproach.[18] Most recently, the former president of the UAW, Gary Jones, pleaded guilty in federal court on June 3, 2020 to racketeering.[19]

An Overview of the Scandals

The corruption at the UAW and selected joint training centers originated in different units of the union and its corporate counterparts, metastasizing into an intricate network of conspiratorial embezzlement facilitated through fraud, money laundering, and falsifying financial disclosures. These orchestrated schemes to chisel union members and corporate-financed coffers had as their motivation a blend of greed and power. A select group of corporate and union officials took it upon themselves to live lavishly at others' expense in violation of labor laws and ethical codes of conduct. [At this time, 15 union and corporate individuals have pled guilty to charges of wrongdoing; in this book, we copiously cite the court-related documents (criminal complaints, plea bargains, indictments, sentencing memoranda, sentencing hearings) filed by US Attorney for the Southern Division of the Eastern District of Michigan and civil Racketeer Influenced and Corrupt Organizations Act (RICO) complaints filed by General Motors, which include information repeated in the aforementioned court documents. The court documents are striking in their characterizations of the conduct of UAW and corporate officials in financial wrongdoing for personal gain.] High-ranking corporate executives apparently concocted a plan to buy influence in the UAW in order to gain favorable and financially beneficial treatment. In other parts of the UAW, union officials separately launched their own schemes to embezzle union funds, tapping the International's treasury and selected UAW Community Action Programs (CAPs). [CAPs are political action committee which, under federal and state election campaign laws, raise money from union rank-and-file on a voluntary basis; these funds may, in turn, be contributed to political candidates running for office within amounts permitted by applicable law].[20]

While personal gain drove much of the misconduct, it did not constitute the entire motivation. Perhaps the most institutionally disconcerting activities involved the apparent attempt by selected corporate executives at FCA/Chrysler, including the late CEO of Fiat, Sergio Marchionne, to use the joint UAW-Chrysler National Training Center (NTC), which was funded by the company, to "buy" influence in the UAW in order to extract concessions in collective bargaining and labor-management relations.[21] More broadly, the training centers at each company (the aforementioned NTC, UAW-GM Center for Human Resources, CHR, and UAW-Ford National Program Center, NPC) had been subsidizing the UAW through a practice of "chargebacks" to the UAW. In short, the centers paid the UAW to cover the compensation of the employees who were assigned to the training programs, with the union charging an additional seven-percent "administrative fee," which, according to the US Attorney's office, amounted to sheer profit for the union. While some of these employees did legitimate work, others were allegedly "ghost" employees who actually worked only for the UAW itself. These chargebacks, as we will show, amounted to hundreds of millions of dollars over time, providing at least a partial subsidy to the UAW to maintain its bureaucracy. As Thomas Adams (2019) has argued in a revealingly titled article "A Tale of Corruption by the United Auto Workers and the Big Three American Automakers," based on the extensive research he had done for his dissertation, the joint training centers had essentially corrupted the relationship between labor and management, substituting cozy labor-management relations for aggressive union member representation.[22]

At this point, based on criminal complaints, indictments, convictions, and extensive news coverage, we know that the assorted illicit activities clustered in three main arenas: (1) the FCA and UAW through its National Training Center (UAW-Chrysler National Training Center, referred hereafter as

NTC); (2) the UAW-GM Center for Human Resources (CHR); and (3) Solidarity House (the UAW's International and Regional headquarters organization), Region 5, and Palm Springs, which intersected somewhat with the NTC scandal. In addition, GM filed a controversial civil RICO suit against FCA, targeting not just individuals but implicating institutions in systemic corruption. A federal judge recently dismissed, but GM filed an amended suit shortly thereafter (August 3, 2020) making additional allegations against FCA and the former president of the UAW, Dennis Williams, involving secret off-shore bank accounts.[23] The same federal judge dismissed the amended case shortly thereafter, but GM plans to appeal to the US Court of Appeals.

Parenthetically, in this mix of activity, the UAW undertook to make major improvements to an existing cottage used by a former international president, for whom it had built an expensive new cottage which has since been put up for sale (see text box on the UAW Black Lake). The UAW financed these improvements with interest on the its strike fund. The strike fund itself is funded by income received from the UAW, including members' dues.

UAW Black Lake

The UAW opened its 1,000-acre Black Lake educational and recreational center in 1970. The center represented a dream of Walter Reuther, who viewed it as mecca for working families. In fact, Reuther and his wife, May, were on their way to Black Lake when they died tragically in a plane crash in May 1970. Their ashes have been scattered on the grounds of Black Lake.

The center includes a 241-room lodging complex, conference-education facilities, a gym, a campground, and an Olympic-sized pool. It also includes a golf course, built in 2000 at the cost of $6 million.[24] It charges user fees but is also subsidized by the UAW.

Black Lake has habitually operated at a deficit. In the five years preceding 2008, it had deficits that totaled $23 million. In 2017, its deficit amounted to $2.8 million.[25] The center is in arrears to the UAW for approximately $61 million.[26]

The UAW subsidizes the center from interest on its sizable strike fund. The UAW estimates the book values of the conference center at $32.5 million and the golf course at $5.4 million.[27]

In 2018, the UAW convention adopted a resolution to build a new cottage for outgoing president Dennis Williams. Construction of the cottage would be supervised by a non-profit Union Building Corporation, which Williams was head of while he was UAW president.

Construction of the new cottage began in 2018, after significant renovations had been made in the existing cottage that was then being used by Williams. The UAW announced that the cottage upgrade and new cottage construction were funded as part of $10 million renovation project for Black Lake approved in 2015.[28]

It has been reported that the US Attorney's office was investigating whether certain upgrades to accommodations at Black Lake, including boats, audio-visual equipment, and other items, might have been paid for by the Detroit 3's joint training centers with the union.[29]

The cottage that was being built for Dennis Williams was first reported in October 2018.[30] Blueprints for the cottage revealed that it included three bedrooms, granite centers, stainless-steel appliances, a wine cooler, and a hidden storage room.

It was reported on June 11, 2020 that the UAW had an offer to buy the new cottage which was listed for almost $1.3 million, pending release of liens on the property.[31] Dennis Williams had used the site of the new cottage as his home address.

The UAW-Chrysler FCA National Training Center

The scandal involving officials affiliated with the FCA and UAW represented an orchestrated effort by high-ranking corporate and union officials to steal funds for personal enrichment and broader organizational objectives. In particular, the high-ranking corporate officers included the late CEO of FCA (Sergio Marchionne) and the Vice President of Employee Relations, Alphons Iacobelli, adopted the strategy in early 2009, before the Fiat-Chrysler merger, of bribing top UAW officers connected with Chrysler in order to promote a more company-friendly labor-management relationship.[32] Marchionne aimed specifically at using this relationship to reduce Chrysler's relative labor-cost structure in order to make the company a more appealing partner for an eventual mega-merger with GM.[33] To execute this strategy, the corporate leaders channeled funds from the UAW-Chrysler National Training Center to union officials to use for personal expenditures on expensive gifts, mortgages, entertainment, jewelry, clothing, home improvements, and travel. Some of the funds were laundered through a charity and a dummy company set up for use by the late International Vice President of the UAW and his girlfriend/spouse, Monica Morgan. The bribes were explicitly intended to make the union officials "fat, dumb, and happy."[34] Eventually, the corporate Vice President of Employee Relations of Chrysler (eventually FCA) couldn't resist involving other corporate officers in an effort to partake of the graft himself on a large scale of embezzlement.

In addition, the FCA-funded National Training Center arranged to make substantial payments to the UAW in the form of "chargebacks," which exceeded $34 million between 2013 and 2018.[35] The chargebacks, which included a seven-percent "administrative fee," reimbursed the union for the salaries of various UAW employees assigned to the training center. Some of these "employees" were allegedly ghost workers who performed no duties. FCA officials involved in this arrangement viewed the chargebacks as a "political gift" to the UAW for which the company would derive benefits in negotiating cost-favorable collective bargaining agreements and resolving grievances in a cost-efficient manner.

We summarize the key elements of this scandal in Table I.1. Excluding the amount of money involved in any potentially problematic "chargebacks," the scandal involved the misuse of well over $4 million in NTC funds. Numerous corporate and union officials with involvement in the NTC exploited their positions for personal gain, in some cases with another ulterior motive. They committed various crimes to facilitate this illegal transfer of wealth, using nefarious means to cover their tracts.

The UAW-GM Center for Human Resources

The joint UAW-GM Center for Human Resources (CHR) became a tempting source of money for three UAW officials to let contracts with vendors for which "kickbacks" were received (Table I.2). In the case of Joe Ashton,

Table I.1 UAW Scandal: FCA and UAW[36]

Dimensions	Description
Narrative	This scandal involving the FCA and UAW, operating principally through the joint UAW-FCA National Training Center, had two related components. The first component involved efforts on the part of UAW and corporate officials to divert NTC funds for their personal use; the second involved a concerted effort by FCA executives to "buy" influence with the UAW to the influence labor-management relations to the financial advantage of the company
Players	Sergio Marchionne, former CEO of FCA, deceased; Alphons Iacobelli, former Vice President of Employee Relations, FCA; General Holiefield, the deceased former UAW International Vice President; Norwood Jewell, former UAW International Vice President; Michael Brown, former FCA Director of Employee Relations; Monica Morgan-Holiefield (UAW vendor and girlfriend/ spouse of General Holiefield); Virdell King, former UAW official; Keith Mickens, former UAW official; Nancy A. Johnson, former UAW official; Jerome Durden, former FCA Financial Analyst
Organizations	UAW Solidarity House; UAW-Chrysler National Training Center; FCA
Time Period	2009–2017
Crimes	Embezzlement; wire and mail fraud; filing false tax returns; conspiracy to violate Labor Management Relations Act; making illegal payments to influence union officials and labor organizations in labor-management relations
Financial Value	Over $4.5 million for personal gain and over $10 million in UAW-FCA NTC "chargebacks" to UAW

Table I.2 UAW Scandal: UAW-GM The East Coast Connection[37]

Dimensions	Description
Narrative	Joe Ashton, former International Vice President, UAW, and two of his assistants conspired with a vendor in the Philadelphia, PA area to grant a fraudulent contract and receive "kickbacks" for payment, which was made by the UAW-GM Center for Human Resources; two other vendor contracts were let for which Grimes and/or Pietrzyk received kickbacks
Players	Joseph Ashton, former UAW International Vice President; Michael Grimes, former UAW administrative assistant; Jeff Pietrzyk, former UAW administrative assistant
Organizations	UAW-GM Center for Human Resources
Time Period	2006–2016
Crimes	Honest services fraud; conspiracy to commit wire fraud and money laundering
Financial Value	>$2 million

the former International Vice President of the UAW in charge of the General Motors department, the crime involved letting a false contract to purchase 58,000 watches to be given to every hourly worker of GM in recognition of quality improvements. The contract was let to Ashton's personal chiropractor who practiced in Philadelphia, PA. In exchange for the $3.9 million contract, paid for by the CHR, Ashton demanded a kickback of $250,000. [The watches were delivered and warehoused, never to be distributed to the rank-and-file.] Ashton's administrative assistants Michael Grimes and Jeff Pietrzyk participated in similar schemes.

UAW Solidarity House, Region 5, and Palm Springs

This segment involved the top leadership of the UAW and three successive directors of Region 5 (see Table I.3). Unlike the other two, it involved the use of UAW members' dues (or at least money from the union's national treasury). Participants sought to finance a lavish lifestyle in which the officials by embezzling from the UAW treasury, UAW-Chrysler-NTC, and UAW Midwest and Southwest Community Action Programs (CAPs) were able to purchase expensive meals, living accommodations, entertainment, and recreation (golf and related accoutrements). They created fake "Master Accounts" at resorts, including the Renaissance Palm Springs Hotel (RPSH), to conceal the purchases. These union officials laundered funds through false accounts which often fraudulently claimed that they were being used to cover legitimate expenses in connection with major leadership training programs sponsored by the former Region 5, which the UAW has just recently closed and folded into two existing regions. The UAW officials direct billed

Table I.3 UAW Scandal: Solidarity House and Region 5[38]

Dimension	Description
Narrative	The crux of this scandal is the systematic embezzlement of union funds to finance a lavish lifestyle that was concealed as part of regular leadership conferences held by Region 5 in Palm Springs, CA. Three successive Region 5 Directors, including Gary Jones, who eventually became UAW president, conspired to channel union-connected funds to selected resorts who paid for meals, entertainment, housing, and recreation by these three officials, plus Dennis Williams and Norwood Jewell. They established "Master Accounts" at these resorts from which the parties could direct bill their expenses, which were falsified to hide their real purpose. Parenthetically, the UAW paid for improvements in the cottage used by former President Williams and to build a new cottage for him, which has since been sold for nearly $1.3 million
Players	Dennis Williams, former UAW President; Gary Jones, former UAW President and Region 5 Director; Norwood Jewell, former International Vice President, UAW; Vance Pearson, former Region 5 Director, UAW; Jim Wells, former Region 5 Director, UAW, deceased) Eugene "Nick" Robinson, former president UAW Midwest CAP
Organizations	UAW Solidarity House; UAW-Chrysler National Training Center; Renaissance Palm Springs Hotel (RPSH), UAW Southwest CAP, UAW Midwest Cap, Loews Coronado Bay Resort, Lodge of Four Seasons; UAW Region 5
Time Period	2009–2017
Crimes	Embezzlement; mail and wire fraud; filing false reports; money laundering; aiding and abetting; conspiracy
Financial Value	Over $1.5 million

the accounts for purchases of goods and services provided by various vendors (restaurants, grocery stores, housing rental agencies).

Organization of the Book

We divide the rest of this book into 12 chapters. Our purpose is to provide some context for assessing the import of the scandals and to evaluate the potential remedies, as well as to discuss what possible impact the events may have had on collective bargaining among the Detroit 3 and the UAW. Chapter One provides historical context and develops the narrative to explain what contributed to a multi-layered scandal of vast proportions. Chapter Two reviews the UAW as an organization, describing how it is governed, its organizational structure, and selected aspects of its administration. In Chapter Three, we examine the UAW's financial situation to show the various pressures the union faced during an economically challenging time period. Chapter Four discusses the relevant laws which regulate the conduct of unions as well as corporate and labor officials engaged in labor-management relations.

In Chapter Five we discuss the emergence and nature of the Detroit 3-UAW joint training programs. Chapter Six addresses the state of the industry in the midst of the Great Recession and concomitant declarations of bankruptcy by GM and Chrysler. In Chapters Seven through Nine we describe the UAW scandal trifurcated into it three main clusters: the UAW-Chrysler NTC (Chapter Seven); Solidarity House, Region 5 and Palm Springs (Chapter Eight); and the UAW-GM CHR (Chapter Nine). Chapter Ten reviews the RICO suit filed by GM against FCA, while Chapter Eleven explores the recent rounds of collective bargaining and the associated financial performance of the Detroit 3. In Chapter Twelve we discuss the alternative approaches to reforming the UAW, including the possibility of a government takeover.

Notes

1 Barnard, J. (2004). *American Vanguard: The United Auto Workers during the Reuther Years, 1935–1970*. Detroit: Wayne State University Press; Brooks, C. (2020, March). The Death and Life of the United Auto Workers. *In These Times*, 24–31.
2 Stieber, J. (1962). *Governing the UAW*. New York: John Wiley and Sons, Inc.; Serrin, W. (1973). *The Company and the Union: The "Civilized" Relationship between General Motors and the United Automobile Workers*. New York: Alfred A. Knopf.
3 Greenhouse, S. (2019). *Beaten Down, Worked Up: The Past, Present, and Future of American Labor*. New York: Alfred A. Knopf; Katz, H.C., MacDuffie, J.P., and Pil, F.K. (2013). Crisis and Recovery in the US Auto Industry: Tumultuous Times for a Collective Bargaining Pacesetter, in H.R. Stanger, P.F. Clark, and A. C. Frost (Eds.) *Collective Bargaining Under Distress: Case Studies of North American Industries*. Champaign, IL: Labor and Employment Relations Association, pp. 45–80.
4 Reuther, V.G. (1976). *The Brothers Reuther and the Story of the UAW/A Memoir*. Boston: Houghton Mifflin Company.
5 Jacobs, J.B. and Cooperman, K.T. (2011). *Breaking the Devil's Pact: The Battle to Free the Teamsters from the Mob*. New York: New York University Press; Estey, M.S., Taft, P., and Wagner, M. (eds.) (1964). *Regulating Union Government*. New York: Harper & Row Publishers; Seidman, J. (1964). Emergence of Concern with Union Government and Administration, in Estey et al., *op. cit.*, pp. 1–27; Levitan, S. A. and Loewenberg, J.J. (1964). The Politics and Provisions of the Landrum-Griffin Act, in Estey et al., *op. cit.*, pp. 28–64.
6 Wall-Howard, P. (2020, July 15). FCA to Change Its Name to Stellantis After Merger with PSA in 2021. *Detroit Free Press*.
7 Adams, T. (2010). *UAW Incorporated: The Triumph of Capital*. PhD Dissertation, Michigan State University; Bickley, J. M. (2008). *Chrysler Corporation Loan Guarantee Act of 1979: Background, Provisions, and Cost*. Congressional Research Service, RL40005, December 17; Cooney, S. (2007). Motor Vehicle Manufacturing Employment: National and State Trends and Issues. Congressional Research Service, RL34297.

8 Cannis, B., Bickley, J.M., Chaikind, H., Pettit, C.A., Purcell, P., Rapaport, C., and Shorter, G. (2009). US Motor Vehicle Industry: Federal Assistance and Restructuring. Congressional Research Service R40003, May 29; Cannis, B. and Yacobucci, B.D. (2010). The US Motor Vehicle Industry: Confronting a New Dynamic in the Global Economy. Congressional Research Service, R41154, March 26; Cooney, op. cit; Cutcher-Gershenfeld, J., Brooks, D., and Mulloy. M. (2015). Inside the Ford-UAW Transformation: Pivotal Events in Valuing Work and Delivering Results. Cambridge, MA: MIT Press; Bickley, op. cit.

9 Goeddeke, F., and Masters, M.F. (2020). The United Auto Workers: From Walter Reuther to Rory Gamble, Perspectives At Work, forthcoming.

10 McAldinden, S., Dziczek, K., and Schwartz, A. (2011, November 29). 2011 Detroit 3–UAW Labor Contract Negotiations. Center for Automotive Research Breakfast Briefing Schoolcraft Community College Livonia, Michigan; McAlinden, S.P. and Chen, Y. (2012, December). After the Bailout: Future Prospects for the US Auto Industry. Ann Arbor, MI: Center for Automotive Research; McAlinden, S. (2015, June 23). Some Mild Commentary and Observations Regarding D3-UAW Bargaining for a New Labor Agreement. Center for Automotive Industry Briefing, Detroit, MI; Schwartz, A.R. (2015, June 23). Leading Up to the 2015 UAW-Detroit Three Talks. Center for Automotive Research Conference. https://www.cargroup.org/wp-content/uploads/2017/02/IB_Jun2015_art_shwartz.pdf.

11 Canis and Yacobucci, op. cit; McAlinden, Dziczek, & Schwartz, op. cit.

12 Canis et al., op. cit.

13 Rattner, S. (2010). Overhaul: An Insider's Account of the Obama Administration's Emergency Rescue of the Auto Industry. Boston: Houghton Mifflin Harcourt.

14 Cutcher-Gershenfeld et al., op. cit.

15 McAlinden, op.cit.

16 US Department of Labor, UAW LM-2 financial disclosure reports filed between 2000 and 2018.

17 Burden, M. and Snell, R. (2017, July 26). Former FCA exec, wife of former UAW VP indicted. *The Detroit News.*

18 Adams, T. (2019, August 19). A Tale of Corruption by the United Auto Workers and the Big Three American Manufacturers, *MR Online*; US Attorney's Office, Eastern District of Michigan (2020, June 3). *Former UAW President Gary Jones Pleads Guilty to Embezzlement*, Racketeering, and Tax Evasion. Press Release; Brooks, *op. cit.*

19 US Attorney, *op cit.*

20 Congressional Research Service. (2018). *The State of Campaign Finance Policy: Recent Developments and Issues for Congress*, R41542, December 13.

21 GM LLC, General Motors Company v. FCA, Alphons Iacobelli, Michael Durden, and Michael Brown, Civil Complaint, November 20, 2019, Case 2: 19-cv-13429, United States District Court Eastern District, Southern Division; GM LLC v. FCA, Dennis Williams, Joseph Ashton, Alphons Iacobelli, Jerome Durden, Michael Brown, First Amended Complaint, Demand for Jury Trial, August 3, 2020, No. 19-cr-13429, United States District Court Eastern District, Southern Division.

22 Adams, 2019, *op. cit.*

23 Lawrence, E.D. and LaReau, J. (2020, July 8). Judge Dismisses GM Racketeering Suit Against FCA. *Detroit Free Press; General Motors LLC v. FCA US LLC* (E.D. Mich. June 23, 2020) Case No. 19-cv-13429; US Sixth Court of Appeals, *General Motors LLC v. FCA US LLC*, July 6, 2020, No. 20-1616; *General Motors LLC v. FCA US LLC* (E.D. Mich. July 8, 2020) Case No. 19-cv-13429.

24 Lawrence, E.D. (2019, January 5). Up North UAW Resort Bleeds Millions, Plans Controversial Lavish Cabin. *Detroit Free Press.*

25 Lawrence, 2019, *op cit.*

26 Ibid.

27 US Department of Labor, UAW 2019 LM-2 Reports.

28 Snell, R. (2019, October 8). Feds Probe Whether Detroit Carmakers Helped Fund Dennis Williams' UAW Cabin. *Detroit News.*

29 Ibid.

30 Ibid.

31 Krisher, T., and White, E. (2020, June 11). UAW Accepts Offer on Up North Lake Home Built For Ex-President. *Detroit Free Press.*

32 GM LLC, General Motors Company v. FCA, Alphons Iacobelli, Michael Durden, and Michael Brown, Civil Complaint, November 20, 2019, Case 2: 19-cv-13429, United States District Court Eastern District, Southern Division; GM LLC v. FCA, Dennis Williams, Joseph Ashton, Alphons Iacobelli, Jerome Durden, Michael Brown, First Amended Complaint, Demand for Jury Trial, August 3, 2020, No. 19-cr-13429, United States District Court Eastern District, Southern Division.

33 Wolfcale, J. (2015, June 10). Sergio Marchionne Wants to Merge with General Motors. *Topspeed.*

34 GM LLC, General Motors Company v. FCA, Alphons Iacobelli, Michael Durden, and Michael Brown, Civil Complaint, November 20, 2019, Case 2: 19-cv-13429, United States District Court Eastern District, Southern Division; GM LLC v. FCA, Dennis Williams, Joseph Ashton, Alphons Iacobelli, Jerome Durden, Michael Brown, First Amended Complaint, Demand for Jury Trial, August 3, 2020, No. 19-cr-13429, United States District Court Eastern District, Southern Division.

35 GM LLC, General Motors Company v. FCA, Alphons Iacobelli, Michael Durden, and Michael Brown, Civil Complaint, November 20, 2019, Case 2: 19-cv-13429, United States District Court Eastern District, Southern Division; GM LLC v. FCA, Dennis Williams, Joseph Ashton, Alphons Iacobelli, Jerome Durden, Michael Brown, First Amended Complaint, Demand for Jury Trial, August 3, 2020, No. 19-cr-13429, United States District Court Eastern District, Southern Division.

36 USA v. Alphons Iacobelli and Nancy A. Morgan, First Superseding Indictment, July 26, 2017, Case No. 17-cr-20406, United States District Court Eastern District Michigan, Southern Division; USA v. Eugene N. Robinson, Plea Bargain, March 2, 2020, Case No. 19-cr-20726, United States District Court Eastern District Michigan, Southern Division; GM LLC v. FCA, Dennis Williams, Joseph Ashton, Alphons Iacobelli, Jerome Durden, Michael Brown, First Amended Complaint, Demand for Jury Trial, August 3, 2020, No. 19-cr-13429, United States District Court Eastern District Michigan, Southern Division; USA v. Nancy A. Johnson, Sentencing Memorandum, No. 17-cr-20406, December 12, 2018, Sentencing Memorandum, United States District Court Eastern District, Michigan, Southern Division; USA v. Michael Brown. Sentencing Memorandum, Case No. 17-cr-20406, October 31, 2018, United States District Court Eastern District, Southern Division; USA v. Nancy A. Johnson, Criminal Complaint, March 14, 2018, Case No. 17-cr-20406, United States District Court Eastern District, Southern Division; USA v. Alphons Iacobelli, Sentencing Memorandum, August 20, 2018, Case No. 17-cr-20407, United States District Court Eastern District, Southern Division; USA v. Keith Mickens, Sentencing Memorandum, Case No. 17-cr-20406, September 31, 2018, United States District Court Eastern District, Southern Division; USA v. Norwood Jewell, Plea Agreement, April 2, 2019, Case No. 19-cr-20146, United States District Court Eastern District,

Southern Division; USA v. Virdell King, Sentencing Memorandum, November 6, 2018, Case No. 17-cr-20406, United States District Court Eastern District, Southern Division.

37 USA v. Joseph Ashton, Criminal Complaint, November 6, 2019, Case 5: 19-cr-20738, United States District Court Eastern District, Southern Division; USA v. Michael Grimes, Plea Agreement, September 3, 2019, Case No. 19-cr-20520, United States District Court Eastern District, Southern Division; USA v. Jeffrey Pietrzyk, Criminal Complaint, Case 2: 19-CR-20630, September 20, 2019, United States District Court Eastern District, Michigan, Southern Division.

38 USA v. Vance Pearson, Criminal Complaint, September 12, 2019, Case No. 2: 19-mj-30488, United States District Court Eastern District, Southern Division; USA v. Eugene N. Robinson, Plea Bargain, March 2, 2020, Case No. 19-cr-20726, United States District Court Eastern District Michigan, Southern Division; USA v. Gary Jones, Criminal Complaint, Second Superseding Information, February 27, 2020, Criminal No. 19–20726, United States District Court Eastern District, Southern Division.

Chapter I

The UAW

An Iconic Union Gripped in Scandal

The United Auto Workers (UAW) has occupied a special place in labor history. It emerged in the economic and political turmoil of the Great Depression from intense struggle that often spilled into violence. After an initial decade of internal strife, Walter Reuther assumed leadership and consolidated power within the union, which became one of the largest and most powerful in modern history.[1] Through Reuther, the UAW negotiated path-breaking collective bargaining agreements (CBAs) with the then-Big 3 (now Detroit 3), promoted broader causes of social justice, such as civil rights for African Americans and other minorities, and established a reputation as an organization committed to high ethical standards.

The tragic death of Walter and May Reuther in a plane crash in May 1970 coincided with the advent of major structural changes in the auto manufacturing industry that would bedevil the UAW and the Detroit 3 for decades to come.[2] A combination of intense global competition, energy crises, neoliberal public policies, uncompetitive labor costs, and outmoded manufacturing processes paved the way to massive disruption.[3] These seismic forces resulted in dwindling market share, plant closures, and job cutbacks, which culled UAW ranks. In this vortex, the UAW and the Detroit 3 negotiated a series of CBAs to address mutual problems, aimed at protecting jobs while helping the companies to become more competitive, especially vis-à-vis the rising foreign-owned transplants in the US.[4] The UAW necessarily made concessions while the Detroit 3 agreed to programs (i.e. the famous or infamous "jobs bank") to protect the economic security of displaced workers. Cooperative arrangements in the form of joint company-UAW training programs grew from the wave concessionary bargaining in the 1980s. The training centers at GM, Ford, and Chrysler/FCA evolved as tax-exempt nonprofit organizations funded by the companies through negotiated formulae to ensure sustainability.[5] To varying degrees, the centers eventually ended up providing the mechanisms for bankrolling corruption and complacent bureaucracy, which proved symbiotic.[6]

Eventually, the immutable thrust of bureaucracy joined the internal dynamics of the UAW to give the training centers a life of their own. Each center became a broad-based social welfare entity, generating vast sums of money whose management lacked adequate transparency or accountability. They proved fertile soil for the emergence of what became a "culture of corruption."[7] This culture metastasized to involve union officials who tapped into the UAW's treasury to support lavish lifestyles.[8] In the case of the joint training program between the UAW and Chrysler (later FCA), it apparently became an instrument used by pernicious corporate executives bent on engineering a more cooperative labor-management relationship to the decided advantage of the company.[9] Thus, one of the Detroit 3 (GM) has recently filed an amended suit against a competitor (FCA), alleging that it became a racketeer-influenced organization through which it inflicted economic damage through illicit conduct.[10] In another instance, at GM, the UAW officials used contracts from its joint training center as a mechanism for shaking down contractors for kickbacks.[11]

To appreciate fully the nature and scope of the scandal which has swept the UAW into disrepute, it is necessary to provide historical context. We trace the milestones which litter the rise and decline of the UAW over its nearly nine-decade existence. In parallel, we review key developments in the union's bargaining with the Detroit 3, underscoring the cyclical and structural vicissitudes of this economically significant industrial sector—motor vehicle and parts manufacturers. Several pivotal points emerge in the organizational and bargaining history of the UAW to create conditions ripe for scandal. None of these plausible explanations, however, excuse the misconduct of guilty union and corporate officials who were motivated by personal greed and hunger for power. At the same time, effective remedies may require institutional reforms above and beyond the imposition of additional financial controls and ethical rules. The narrative we develop through our analysis of the multi-faceted scandal surrounding selected UAW and corporate officials provides a framework to evaluate the realm of remedies available.

In writing this book, we have reviewed the extensive public records on the federal prosecutors' criminal filings, the civil Racketeer Influenced and Corrupt Organizations (RICO) suit filed by GM against FCA, union financial disclosure reports filed with the US Department of Labor, available financial reports filed by the Detroit 3 and UAW training centers, news reports, and other journalistic and scholarly writings on relevant topics. Our analysis of the evidence has enabled us to build a narrative which describes the origin and metastasizing of the misconduct to envelop a five-star cast of officials. The narrative has centered on how the motivations of personal greed and power led well-placed officials to breach the law. At the same time, a few corporate executives had decided to leverage the monies available in their company's joint training center with the UAW (UAW-Chrysler NTC) to corrupt the institutional integrity of both collective bargaining and labor-management relations. To a certain extent, the scandal unfolded in a disjointed and uncoordinated fashion across separate units of the UAW and the jointly run training centers (at FCA and

GM). However, to some extent the misconduct intersected among politically ambitious individuals in different units in what appears to be a concerted effort to curry favor to secure reciprocal favoritism in the next set of UAW elections for the UAW International's presidency. Also, selected corporate officials used illegal means to gain influence within the UAW to their company's advantage. Moreover, the cozy relationship that emerged between the companies and the UAW has raised doubt about whether financial interdependence is consonant with the genuinely independent labor movement.[12]

The Rise and Decline of the UAW

The United Auto Workers emerged in 1935 when it was formally chartered by the American Federation of Labor (AFL), after more than a decade of unsuccessful attempts to organize the nascent industry.[13] Its inception coincided with the enactment of the National Labor Relations Act (NLRA) of that same year, which granted workers in the private sector outside of rail and air transportation the right to form unions and bargain collectively, setting a landmark in the march of labor rights (see Table 1.1 for a timeline of major developments in the rise and decline of the UAW). The largely craft-based AFL appointed Francis Dillon as the first president of the embryonic UAW entity, which had about 30,000 members when it convened its inaugural constitutional convention in South Bend, Indiana in 1936, a convocation attended by Walter Reuther.[14]

At its first convention, the assembled UAW delegates elected Homer Martin president while Reuther was chosen for the International Executive Board (IEB). In this pivotal year, the UAW embarked upon a deft campaign to organize General Motors (GM), focusing on its major manufacturing site in Flint, Michigan. A cadre of militant activists engaged in a sit-down strike in late 1936 to force a recalcitrant GM leadership to grant formal recognition. In 1936, parenthetically, the UAW had affiliated with the newly formed Committee on Industrial Organizations (a precursor to the Congress of Industrial Organizations, CIO), which concentrated on unionizing industrial rather than craft workers. The tense and episodically violent sit-downs resulted in the eventual recognition of the UAW in 1937, which was followed closely by similar action at Chrysler. The UAW's ranks swelled immediately thereafter to roughly 300,000 by 1939. In 1937, the Battle of the Overpass at the Ford Rouge occurred. Reuther and other UAW leaders suffered injuries during this violent encounter with the company's private police force. Photos of this beating were published nationally, resulting in public support for the union and auto workers. What transpired at the Overpass on the River Rouge has long symbolized the virulent hostility of American management toward union representation.

Between 1937 and 1939, vicious infighting occurred in the UAW, with the Martin-led Progressive Caucus vying for power with the Unity Caucus,

Table 1.1 Timeline of Key UAW-Related Events[15]

Date	Event
Pre-1935	Selected attempts to organize the emerging auto manufacturing indus-try; United Automobile, Aircraft, and Vehicle Workers Union has 45,000 members in 1920
1935	AFL charters United Auto Workers; Francis Dillon appointed pre-sident; National Labor Relations Act passed
1936–37	UAW constitutional convention elected Homer Martin president; UAW engages in Flint sit-down strike; GM recognizes UAW; Walter Reuther elected to UAW International Executive Board (IEB); Chrysler recognizes UAW; UAW joins Congress of Industrial Unions (CIO)
1938	Unity Caucus (Thomas-Reuther) and Progressive Caucus (Martin) vie for power; Reuther named director of General Motors department; Battle of the Overpass
1939	Competing UAW conventions held (UAW-AFL and UAW-CIO); AFL faction elects Martin president; CIO faction elects R.J. Thomas president
1940	UAW-CIO wins recognition to represent GM workers; Reuther elected International Vice President (VP)
1941	Ford recognizes UAW
1945–46	Reuther leads 113-day strike against GM fighting for 30% wage increase; settles for 18.5% hike
1946	Reuther elected president of the UAW; Reuther Caucus has eight members of the 22-person IEB
1947	Taft-Hartley Act passed
1948	Walter Reuther shot in assassination attempt at his home
1949	UAW strikes Chrysler for 104 days
1950	Treaty of Detroit
1952	Reuther elected president of CIO
1955	AFL-CIO merged; George Meany elected president
1959	Labor-Management Reporting and Disclosure Act (Landrum-Griffin) passed
1961	UAW strikes Ford for two weeks
1963	Walk to Freedom in Detroit; March on Washington; UAW Staff Council formed
1964	Civil Rights Act passed
1967	UAW strikes Ford for 66 days
1968	UAW disaffiliated with AFL-CIO; Teamsters and UAW form Alliance for Labor Action; Revolutionary Union Movement formed
1970	Reuther dies in plane crash; Leonard Woodcock becomes president; UAW strikes GM for 67 days
1973	Organization of the Petroleum Exporting Countries (OPEC) oil embargo
1976	UAW strikes Ford for 28 days
1977	Doug Fraser elected president of UAW

(Continued)

Table 1.1 (Cont.)

Date	Event
1979	UAW negotiates lucrative contract with GM; Congress passes $1.2 billion loan guarantee for Chrysler
1979–1981	UAW-Chrysler negotiate three rounds of concessions, UAW membership peaks at over 1.5 million
1981	UAW rejoins AFL-CIO; President Reagan fires striking air traffic controllers (PATCO)
1982	UAW-GM negotiate contract providing for company-funded joint training program, precursor of the Center for Human Resources (CHR)
1983	Owen Bieber elected president of UAW; UAW strikes Caterpillar for 205 days
1985	Canadian division of UAW separates and forms independent Canadian Auto Workers
1993	North American Free Trade Agreement (NAFTA) passed
1995	Stephen Yokich elected president of UAW
1998	UAW strikes selected GM plants for 54 days
2001	US dips into recession
2002	Ron Gettelfinger elected UAW president
2003	Energy crisis
2007	UAW strikes GM for two days
2007–2009	US sustains deepest post-World War II recession
2007	UAW negotiates Voluntary Employee Beneficial Association (VEBA) with Detroit 3
2009	Chrysler and GM file for bankruptcy and exit bankruptcy; receive $85 billion in federal assistance; UAW negotiates new contracts with Detroit 3
2010	Bob King elected president of UAW; launches campaign to organize the foreign-owned auto transplants in US
2014	Workers defeat UAW in bargaining recognition at Volkswagen (VW) plant in Chattanooga, TN plant; Dennis Williams elected president of UAW; constitutional convention raises dues 25%
2015	UAW negotiates first round of contracts with Detroit 3 post-bankruptcy
2017	First media reports on federal investigation of UAW scandal appear
2018	UAW elects Gary Jones president; constitutional convention increases salaries of members of the IEB
2019	UAW strikes GM for 40 days; Gary Jones granted a paid leave; shortly thereafter resigns from the UAW; Rory Gamble elected president of the UAW by IEB; Gamble announces financial reforms
2020	Unite Workers for Democracy launch grass-roots campaign to hold special convention to enact the direct election of IEB members; fails to gain sufficient signatures but relaunches effort; former UAW president Gary Jones charged on February 27 with conspiracy to embezzle union funds and aid racketeering activity; US Attorney says a government takeover of the UAW is an option on the table; Jones plead guilty on June 3, 2020

which included the Reuther brothers (Walter, Roy, and Victor). In 1937, at the union's convention in Milwaukee, the union chose Martin as president, but the Unity Caucus won two vice presidencies. Eventually, the split between the factions led Martin to suspend five Unity Caucus members from the IEB, leaving only himself and R.J. Thomas as members of the board. Sidney Hillman and Philip Murray of the national CIO, neither of whom was fond of Martin, effectively placed the UAW under receivership and reinstated the suspended officers (three of whom had been expelled). A four-person committee, including Murray, Hillman, and Martin, ran the union under the new arrangement.

In October 1938, the Unity Caucus members learned that Martin had been bargaining secretly with Harry Bennett (Head of Ford's Service Department) and Henry Ford. The two Ford leaders tried to convince Martin to affiliate with the AFL in exchange for the company's recognizing the UAW. In January 1939, the UAW IEB named Thomas acting president and Martin resigned in protest.

Neither the Unity Caucus nor the Martin Progressive faction gave up the quest for power, with the two sides holding competing UAW conventions in 1939: UAW-AFL and the UAW-CIO. At UAW-AFL convocation, the delegates chose Martin as president while the CIO affiliate selected R.J. Thomas. It also named Walter Reuther head of the GM department.

Eventually, the UAW-CIO won recognition as the bargaining representative under certification-election procedures established by the NLRA. Bennett and Ford, however, rewarded Martin with a consolation prize of sorts, giving him a house. This practice evidently became more common during this early period, as Bennett is quoted as saying that "This business of giving people homes became quite a thing for us ... We built over 60 houses for people after the Wagner Act [NLRA of 1935] was passed."[16] Collusion between corporate executives and selected UAW officials had thus emerged, with the glue being the company's ability to offer something of tangibly significant value. It could not then have been imagined that history might repeat itself many decades later, albeit in a more contemporaneous fashion.

During its formative years the UAW, as Victor Reuther wrote (1976), basically fought wars on two fronts. First, as discussed, it confronted a lot of centrifugal infighting, which lasted until Walter Reuther was able to consolidate power via the Reuther Caucus (later to be known as the Administrative Caucus). Second, the economic mobilization occasioned by World War II forced the union to find a delicate balance between representing the auto workers while serving the nation's insatiable demand for war-related materials produced by the workers behind the arsenal of democracy.[17] The UAW, along with other unions affiliated with the AFL and CIO, had pledged not to strike during the war in order to fulfill the nation's manufacturing needs in waging war in Europe and the Pacific. In addition to the wartime effects, this no-strike pledge had far-reaching consequences in the post-war development of labor relations.

As the nation emerged victorious in 1945 against the Axis forces, it faced a torrent of pent-up economic pressures to transition from a war-time to peace-time workforce. Between 1941 and 1945, with the economy operating under government wage and price controls, price increases had vastly outpaced wage hikes, thus reducing workers' real income. Demand to catch up rose significantly as the nation adapted to a peace-time economy. The UAW had little choice but to address the growing frustration over the inability of wages to keep pace with inflation. As the head of the GM department, Walter Reuther occupied a prime position to lead such a fight.

In the war years, Reuther gained national attention for his bold proposals for upscaling the manufacturing sector to mass produce war material, which piqued corporate titans and other anti-union forces because it represented an intrusion by labor into the managerial prerogative of making production decisions. At the close of the war, he exploited his prominence to espouse an equally bold proposal to raise wages by 30 percent in the upcoming round of contract negotiations with GM. Reuther took the novel approach of arguing that the auto companies could not only afford to pay the increased wages but also had the ability to do so without raising prices. Reuther linked the interests of the overlapping groups of workers and consumers to bolster his bargaining proposal, which became a precursor to the emerging model of bargaining for the common good. Raising wages would give auto workers more money to buy consumer goods such as automobiles while keeping prices down would further stimulate sales, creating a win-win for auto producers and workers.

The negotiations with GM reached a predictable impasse, which led to a major strike that lasted 113 days. Businesses inside and outside auto exploited the hardships suffered by the strikers to negotiate agreements for less than 30 percent increases. Workers at Ford and Chrysler, for example, settled for between 18 and 18.5 percent increases (see Table 1.2 for a timeline of key bargaining settlements over time). These settlements undercut the strikers, impelling Reuther to settle for a similar 18.5 percent hike at GM. Nonetheless, the UAW demonstrated its resolve and willingness to engage in sustained battle to improve the lot of workers. It matched its willingness to mobilize economically with rising political engagement to pursue an ambitious agenda of social change.

Reuther's growing prominence in the UAW catapulted him into the presidency of the union at the 10th constitutional convention in 1946. He defeated Thomas by a narrow 112-vote margin. Thomas became an International Vice President, and his supporters won 14 of 22 seats on the IEB. While Reuther had the power as president to appoint staff, his lack of a governing majority created complications in administering the UAW. At the 1948 convention, Reuther's ongoing efforts to consolidate power paid off as members of his caucus won a majority of IEB positions.

Table 1.2 Selected Developments in UAW – Detroit 3 Collective Bargaining[18]

Date	Development
1937	GM and Chrysler recognize UAW
1941	Ford recognized UAW
1941–1945	AFL and CIO made no-strike pledge during WW II
1945–1946	UAW strikes GM for 113 days; seeks 30% wage increase; settlements between 18–18.5% increase
1949	Non-contributory pension plan created
1950	Treaty of Detroit: Annual Improvement Factor (AIF); cost-of-living allowance (COLA) established; half Blue Cross/Blue Shield premiums paid by company
1955	AFL-CIO merge
1958	AIF and COLA improvements; health insurance and Supplemental Unemployment Benefits (SUB) improved; Reuther introduces proposal for profit-sharing
1961	Medical insurance for employees paid fully by company
1964	AIF and wage increases: COLA improvements; life and disability insurance paid for by company
1967	UAW strikes Ford; COLA capped at 21 cents for contract; prescription drug plan established
1970	UAW strikes GM for 67 days; wages increased; COLA cap removed; 30-and-out retirement; benefits improved
1973	Oil embargo; dental plan; wage increases
1976	Wage increases; vision care; hearing aid program
1979	Wages increased; benefits improved; SUB improved
1979–1980	Chrysler receives $1.2 billion loan guarantee; UAW negotiates three rounds of concessions
1982	Wages kept at current levels; COLA continued by three adjustments delayed by 18 months; joint training programs established; profit-sharing and Guaranteed Income Stream established
1984	Wages increased; COLA continued; performance bonus for senior employees
1987	Base hour rates increased; COLA continued; benefits improved; hospice and generic drug programs established
1990	Wages increased; COLA continued; benefits improved
1993	Base wages increased; profit sharing made available to new hires
1999	Lump-sum $1,350 paid immediately; COLA continued; 67 paid holidays in contract
2003	Lump-sum payment of $3,000; 3% performance bonus
2007	Lump-sum payment of $3,000; 3% and 4% performance bonuses; COLA discontinued for entry level; VEBA established for retiree healthcare; two-tier wage system established; parties cap lower-paid tier at 20% of workforce; 66 paid holidays in contract
2009	GM and Chrysler enter and exit bankruptcy; bonuses and COLA suspended; Jobs Banks program discontinued; wellness program established; caps lifted on hiring lower-paid tier workers until 2015

Between 1948 and 1970, Reuther led the UAW through the cyclical churns of the auto industry, negotiating CBAs which included precedent-settings provisions to increase wages and benefits while providing for extended economic security. It negotiated an Annual Improvement Factor (AIF) to tie workers' wage increases partly to increases in productivity; cost-of-living-allowances; medical, vision, and dental care; defined benefit pension plans; supplemental unemployment benefits; and plentiful paid holidays and vacation time. The UAW used its bargaining clout, which included a willingness to strike as needed (which was done judiciously but frequently during the Reuther-led years as it grew to nearly 1.5 million-strong in number).

The UAW used its position to advance not only the economic lot workers and but also broader social justice. It played a vital role in the civil rights movement, financing various marches under the direction of Dr. Martin Luther King. In this regard, the UAW helped orchestrate the Freedom March on Detroit and the March on Washington in 1963. As Reuther fortified his base of power in the union through the Reuther Caucus, which evolved into the Administrative Caucus, he also facilitated the merger between the AFL and CIO in the mid-1950s and attempted to move the federation toward a more proactive approach on organizing and politics.

Though the Administrative Caucus dominated the internal governance of the UAW, it did not eliminate dissent or division. The UAW experienced the racial and social tensions of the 1960s, particularly among African-American auto workers who fought for a larger voice in the overwhelmingly white power structure. Chapters of the Revolutionary Union Movement (RUM) sprang up at various plants to fight against racial discrimination and for inclusiveness. Reuther, at the same time, grew increasingly disenchanted with the conservatism of the AFL-CIO under the curmudgeonly George Meany, and disaffiliated with the federation in 1968. Shortly thereafter, the UAW formed a seemingly unholy Alliance for Labor Action with the corruption-tarnished International Brotherhood of Teamsters (IBT), a conjoin that survived less than three years.

To the very end, Reuther stood at the forefront of the labor movement in the United States—indeed, on a global scale. He chided corporate executives for their timidity and backwardness; advised presidents; marched with civil rights leaders and demonstrators; advocated what were at the time heretical bargaining proposals, such as profit-sharing; and provoked competing passions. Reuther represented a formidable force who challenged the status quo, leading US Senator Barry Goldwater to proclaim in 1958 that "Walter Reuther and the UAW-CIO are a more dangerous menace ... than anything Soviet Russia might do to America."[19]

The growth of the UAW from a 30,000-member union in the mid-1930s to one of well over 1 million by the late 1950s corresponded with rising apprehension about organized labor's role in society. By the mid-1950s, unions had organized nearly one-third of the US workforce, displaying a willingness to strike employers in pursuit of bargaining objectives. In some industries, such as auto, steel, rail, and trucking, strikes could inflict major economic hardship on a national scale. With expanded economic strength, a few unions betrayed nontrivial pockets of corruption and abuse of power. Revelations of such untoward practices led lawmakers to enact laws to curb union power, including the Labor Management Relations Act of 1947 (known commonly as Taft-Hartley).

Political pressures mounted in the 1950s to ferret out corruption in unions, causing the US Senate to launch a major inquiry into the topic through the Select Committee on Improper Activities in the Labor or Management Field, which held vast hearings in the years between 1957 and 1959. Chaired by Senator John L. McClellen of Arkansas, with John F. Kennedy serving as one of his Democratic colleagues and Robert F. Kennedy as the committee's chief counsel, the Select Committee uncovered evidence of corrupt practices in several unions, most notably the IBT.[20] In the course of the committee's hearing, it heard testimony from Walter Reuther, as Republican members, including Senate Goldwater, wanted the UAW investigated, particularly regarding matters relating to the UAW's strike against a plumbing manufacturer.

Reuther appeared before the Select Committee on March 28, 1958, emphatically declaring that UAW was a "clean" and democratic union, notwithstanding its critics' claims to the contrary. To demonstrate just how confident he was of his own personal integrity, Reuther voluntarily disclosed his income returns for his years in leadership at the UAW. Reuther noted that he had pushed the AFL-CIO to adopt a strong code of ethical practices in 1957 similar to the one which the UAW had implemented. The UAW also established an independent Public Review Board (PRB) in that same year to hear appeals of members who had suffered adverse decisions in the union.

While testifying, Reuther addressed a little-known topic of interest to a few members of the committee, namely, the UAW's so-called "flower fund."[21] UAW leaders in the Administrative Caucus used this fund to raise money from union officers and administrative staff on a "voluntary" basis to support their efforts to secure election and re-election to union office. By law, the union could not use monies from its treasury for such purposes. Reuther unabashedly justified the fund and its congruence with the ethos of a democratic and corrupt-free union, stressing it was a voluntary program that does not involve dues money.

In 1968, arguably standing at the apex of the UAW's national influence, both economically and politically, Walter Reuther looked fondly upon the upcoming round of contract negotiations in the 1970. After contentious bargaining in the midst of a mild economic downturn in 1967, when inflation was gaining steam, the UAW had struck Ford while each of the domestic producers began to feel the heat of competition from foreign imports, after decades of unparalleled American dominance. Reuther noted that the auto companies had recovered from the downturn and expected them to be flush with profits by 1970. He admonished the corporate executives to lubricate the zippers to their financial coffers because the UAW stood ready to claim the workers' fair share. Reuther drew the battle lines clearly, setting the stage for hard bargaining.

In May 1970, Walter Reuther and his wife May died tragically in a plane crash on their way to Black Lake, a "model" education and recreation center that Reuther had dotingly nursed into being as a symbol of labor's commitment to an enlightened working class in America. His death occurred when the nation was in the midst of a politically divisive war in Vietnam and a sea change in cultural and social norms. Reuther's passing left both a huge leadership vacuum in organized labor and a remarkable legacy.

Nine UAW presidents have served since 1970. From Leonard Woodcock, who assumed the rein after Reuther's untimely death, to Rory Gamble, who took over in late 2019 on the heels of the forced resignation of scandal-tarnished Gary Jones, who pled guilty to criminal charges of embezzlement and racketeering in June 2020, the UAW's leadership has presided over a period of continual decline.[22] Both the Detroit 3 and UAW itself have suffered from torrents of foreign competition, the rise of employment in the non-union foreign-owned auto transplants, successive energy crises, increased governmental regulations, and free-trade agreements which encouraged imports and the offshoring of jobs.[23] To deal with these challenges, the UAW and Detroit 3 engaged in several rounds of concessionary bargaining in the 1980s and 2007–2011 recession era. In the 1980s, each of the Detroit 3 negotiated ambitious, company-funded joint training programs with the UAW to improve productivity, quality, and labor-management relationships (the joint programs evolved into the UAW-GM Center for Human Resources, CHR; the UAW-Chrysler National Training Center, NTC; and the UAW-Ford National Program Center, NPC). These independent, non-profit entities morphed, as we will show, into broader social welfare organizations which operated with limited transparency and supervision. To varying degrees, the companies also experimented with new manufacturing systems and collaborative approaches toward bargaining, exemplified by the interest-based bargaining (IBB) model used between Ford and the UAW.[24]

During the 50 post-Reuther years, the companies and union confronted critical junctures in which the very fate of the industry was in doubt. Suffering a severe downturn in sales along with bloated labor costs, Chrysler received a $1.2 billion federal loan guarantee as a life support in 1979.[25] It negotiated three rounds of concessions with the UAW in the two following years to trim labor costs. In 2009, after slumping sales, plummeting revenues, and closed lines of credit, Chrysler and GM entered bankruptcy, receiving over $85 billion in taxpayer-funded assistance to avoid liquidation.[26] Ford had cleverly escaped a similar bankruptcy fate by securing a massive loan earlier, which leveraged the company lock, stock, and barrel.

The rise and fall of the UAW, as shown in Figure 1.1, has mirrored the twin fates of the US auto industry and organized labor. Membership climbed rapidly in the two decades after its inception to well over 1 million members and rose to a peak of over 1.5 million in the late 1970s. A significant downturn in the auto industry, occasioned by energy crises and concomitant recessions in that time period, caused sizable drops in sales and employment. In the midst of this turbulence, foreign competition accelerated, both in terms of imports of vehicles and production of cars among foreign-owned transplants, the first of which was established by VW in 1978 in Westmoreland, Pennsylvania.

As revealed in Figure 1.2, the Detroit 3's share of the motor vehicle sales market dropped in the 1970s and 1980s. In 1950, only slightly more than 21,000 foreign imports were sold in the US. By 1977, that figure had risen to over two million. In 1986, foreign imports and sales of vehicles produced by foreign transplants stood at 4.8 million. GM's market share in particular dropped from around 45 percent in 1980 to about 28 percent by the turn of the twentieth century.

While foreign competition mounted, employment in the US industry fluctuated widely (Figure 1.3). Between 1980 and 2003, the industry shed 600,000 jobs; in the meantime, employment in foreign-owned transplants climbed to 300,000. Indeed, the US domestic industry had become significantly foreign, a trend magnified when Chrysler merged first with Daimler and then Fiat. The foreign transplants have remained thoroughly non-union, despite repeated attempts to organize targeted sites by the UAW. Any attempt to unionize the transplants has provoked intense opposition, with opponents condemning the UAW for having rendered the Detroit 3 obsolete.

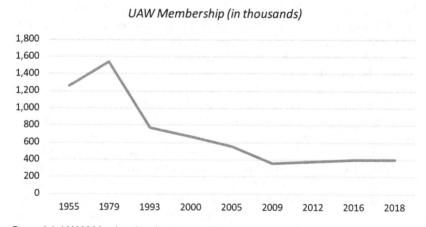

Figure 1.1 UAW Membership (in thousands)
Source: Adams 2010; Serrin 1973; Masters 1997; US Department of Labor LM-2 financial disclosure forms 2000 through 2018.

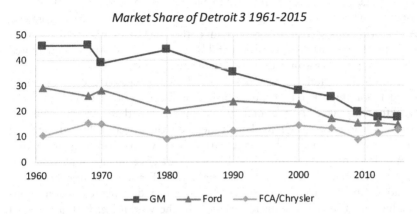

Figure 1.2 Market Share of Detroit 3 1961–2015
Source: McAlinden 2015; Schwartz 2015.

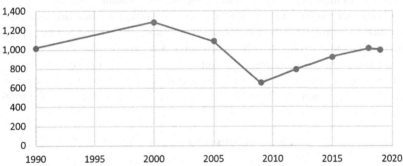

Figure 1.3 US Employment in Motor Vehicle and Parts Manufacturing 1990–2019 (in thousands)
Source: US Bureau of Labor Statistics

In response to stiff competition and changing consumer preferences, the Detroit 3 had not only had to pare labor costs but also shift the mix of product manufactured.[27] In 1979, the Detroit 3, while capturing close to 80 percent of the market in sales, was selling vastly more cars (in sheer number) than light trucks. By 2003, with combined market share having fallen to just above 60 percent, the companies shifted from selling cars (volume-wise) to light trucks. While light trucks comprised less than 27 percent of total vehicle sales in 1979, they amounted to 65 percent in 2003.

To a large extent, the Detroit 3 had yielded the passenger car market to foreign competitors, shifting to the more profitable light-truck segment. Along with this change in product mix, the companies relocated much of their production to non-US sites, notably Mexico, a development facilitated by the North American Free Trade Agreement signed in 1992.

As noted, the fall of the UAW has reflected a wider trend across organized labor (Figure 1.4). Union density, or the rate of membership in the workforce, peaked in the mid-1950s, with more than one-third of the workers belonging to unions. Union members then overwhelmingly worked in the private sector; public sector bargaining laws had yet to gain traction at any level of government, though pockets of government-employee labor representation had nonetheless materialized.[28] Tracked for more than six decades, union density has continually marched downward. Union membership has dropped to only 10.4 percent of the workforce, with a mere 6.4 percent in the private sector having joined the ranks. In the process, public sector workers have climbed to nearly one-half of overall union membership. Moreover, the absolute number of union members has continually shrunk from its peak of over 20 million in the early 1980s to less than 15 million in 2019.

With the decline in union ranks has come a commensurate fall in strikes, across all industries except the public sector. The number of major strikes, involving bargaining units of 1,000 or more employees, has declined precipitously (Figure 1.5). As a point in comparison, the United States experienced 381 major strikes in 1970, when the UAW struck GM for 67 days. In that year, a total of almost 2.47 million workers participated in major strikes, which resulted in nearly 52.8 million idled days of work. Fast forward to 2019, when 49,000 UAW workers struck GM for 40 days, the total

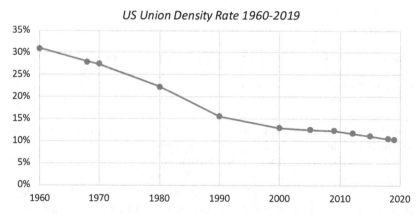

Figure 1.4 US Union Density Rate 1960–2019
Source: Hirsch and MacPherson 2003; www.unionstats.com; Mayer 2004.

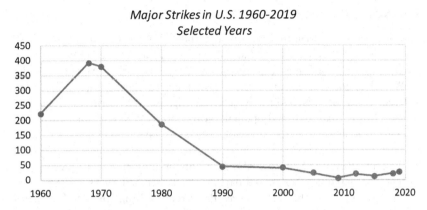

Figure 1.5 Major Strikes in US 1960–2019 Selected Years
Source: US Bureau of Labor Statistics

number of major strikes stood at 25 with fewer than 426,000 workers involved, causing a loss of about 3.25 million days of work. The strike has dwindled as a viable economic instrument for unions, and the overall impact of an auto strike has similarly dropped as the auto industry has shrunk. In 1970, for example, GM had more than 400,000 hourly workers. That number, as suggested, had tumbled to under 50,000 by 2019, which is at a level significantly above the depths of the Great Recession.

In sum, the UAW has had a tumultuous history, closely tied to the fates of the auto industry in general and Detroit 3 in particular. It has seen swift rises in power with equally rapid shrinkage in ranks. The influx of foreign-produced products and the concomitant growth in non-union employment among the transplants has eroded the union's presence and stature. Absent any success in organizing the transplants, the UAW has had to address the competitive disadvantage the Detroit 3 have in terms of labor costs vis-à-vis the transplants. This reality has encouraged the companies to move production to lower-cost locations, such as Mexico. While the UAW has, perforce, organized more in non-auto industries, such a gaming, higher education, and the public sector, its inability to expand in the auto industry has sapped its traditional base of power and identity.

Yet, notwithstanding these challenges and shortcomings, the UAW always had its reputation as a corruption-free and ethical union whose leaders worked tirelessly to improve the lot of working people. It stood in sharp contrast to the corrupted unions exposed in the McClellan hearings, especially the IBT, which had left an indelible scar on organized labor in the US. All of this iconic reverence, however, has collapsed under the weight of revelations of widespread misconduct and abuse of power.

The Scandal Breaks

The veneer of incorruptibility covering the UAW crumbled in July 2017 when federal prosecutors filed charges against officials of the UAW and FCA for the illicit use of funds from the UAW-Chrysler NTC.[29] At the time, the UAW vehemently condemned the wrongdoers, declaring that these were isolated cases of misconduct which ran against the norm at Solidarity House. More than two-and-one-half years later, 15 UAW and corporate officials have been indicted for violating labor law, embezzlement, fraud, racketeering, and reporting requirements to government agencies, include the Internal Revenue Service (IRS). Most of these officials have pled guilty, with several having either served part or all of their jail terms.

On July 26, 2017, the *Detroit Free Press* reported that the US Attorney's office in Eastern Michigan has charged a former FCA executive, Alphons Iacobelli, and the widow of the former International Vice President of the UAW, General Holiefield, who was director of the Chrysler department, which had joint responsibility for the UAW-Chrysler NTC, with embezzlement.[30] We refer to the various incidents of criminal misconduct (either alleged or pled guilty to) by 15 individuals affiliated with the UAW or FCA, plus the others who are implicated by criminal complaints, as the collective UAW scandal, recognizing that selected corporate officers were also involved. The scandal includes several different organizational parts and sets of individuals which are clustered in three spheres of activity: (1) the UAW and Chrysler/FCA, including their NTC; (2) the UAW-GM CHR; and (3) the UAW International's Solidarity House and Region 5, which includes 17 western and southwestern states (see Table 1.3). Millions of dollars were involved in the overt acts of criminal conduct, with money taken from three sources: (1) the NTC and CHR, both of which are financed by the companies (FCA and GM, respectively); (2) the UAW's treasury; and (3) the Community Action Programs (CAPs) associated with Region 5 of the UAW. [CAPs are provided for under the UAW's constitution to promote the economic and social welfare of members and the general public through political action. Region 5, which has since been dissolved by the UAW in early 2020, sponsored a Midwest CAP and Southwestern CAP, both of which serve as political action committees (PACs), as defined under the federal election laws. PACs are permitted to raise money on a voluntary basis from union members and their families to be spent for electioneering purposes, including contributions, within specified limits, to candidates for office. Federal law permits a union to use its treasury monies to finance the operations of PACs, or, in the case of the UAW, the CAPs.]

The overt wrongdoing in the UAW-Chrysler NTC basically involved the embezzlement of NTC funds for personal gain, with a corollary objective to bend labor-management relations to the competitive advantage of FCA (or so it is alleged). At UAW-GM, the overt acts involved shaking down

Table 1.3 Three Clusters of Criminal Misconduct[31]

Cluster	Crimes	Individuals	Amount
UAW-Chrysler/ FCA and NTC	Embezzlement, fraud, violation of labor law, racketeering (civil)	N.J. Adams M. Brown J. Durden G. Holiefield A. Iacobelli N. Jewell V. King S. Marchionne K. Mickens M. Morgan-Holiefield D. Williams	>$4.5 million
UAW-GM CHR	Embezzlement, bribery, fraud	J. Ashton M. Grimes J. Pietrzyk	>$2 million
UAW Solidarity House, Region 5, and Region 5 CAPs	Embezzlement, fraud, racketeering	G. Jones V. Pearson E. Robinson D. Williams	>$1.5 million

vendors for "kickbacks" and covering up the wrongdoing. The third cluster pertained to the embezzlement of the union treasury and CAP funds for personal gain. Based on the criminal complaints and guilty pleas, the amount of money corrupted has exceeded $8 million.

Three other problematic sets of activities are superimposed on these overt incidents where money was stolen for personal use. First, as suggested above, GM alleges FCA executives attempted to "buy" favors from UAW officials in order rebalance labor-management relations to the company's financial advantage.[32] The aforementioned GM RICO lawsuit against FCA has alleged that selected FCA executives, including the late CEO of Fiat (Sergio Marchionne), channeled NTC funds to UAW officials (and selected associates) to gain concessions in CBAs and day-to-day labor-management relations. GM has argued that the FCA leadership had attempted to bribe these concessions which would better position the latter company as an attractive merger partner with the former. Fiat's CEO, Sergio Marchionne, had long argued that there was excess capacity and redundant use of resources in the auto industry, which made the case for corporate consolidations compelling.[33]

Second, the corporate-funded joint training centers (NTC, CHR, and UAW-Ford's National Program Center, NPC) arguably subsidized the UAW by paying the union "chargebacks" to cover the compensation of UAW employees assigned to the training centers. The US Attorney's office has charged that some of these assigned employees were actually "ghost" employees who did no work for the training centers. Adams has argued that the centers fostered cozy relationships between labor and management that jeopardized the institutional independence and integrity of the union.[34]

Finally, the UAW refurbished a cabin at its Black Lake educational and training center for use by the then-UAW International president, Dennis Williams, notwithstanding the fact that Black Lake was operating under financial stress.[35] Moreover, the UAW spent money to build a new cottage for Williams' use that cost the UAW nearly $1.3 million. Objections to these expenditures, once reported by the news media, have resulted in the UAW's putting the new $1.3 million cottage with several acres of land up for sale.

At this time, as noted, 15 individuals have been charged with criminal misconduct, all of whom have pled guilty (see Table 1.4). They include a UAW International President, three International Vice Presidents, two Regional Directors, and a UAW CAP director, plus several corporate officials, including the former Vice President of Employee Relations of FCA. Eleven of these individuals have been sentenced to jail, with three awaiting sentencing. The US Attorney's office has indicated that its investigation is still ongoing and that it is receiving tips from UAW ranks on further evidence of wrongdoing.

The Narrative

The evidence of widespread wrongdoing at the UAW and FCA involves a complex set of facts and activities, with concerted efforts to conceal the misuse of funds and to abuse power.

Notwithstanding the intricate measures taken to cover up illegal and unethical behavior, it is possible to construct a relatively straightforward narrative of what when wrong.

First, personal greed, coupled with abuse of power, motivated the guilty parties at the UAW-GM CHR. The participating UAW officials shook down vendors to extract a price for forwarding business to them.

Second, at UAW-Chrysler NTC, corporate officials apparently attempted to bribe union officials to extract concessions that would benefit the company financially. In the process, a few corporate officials must have found the prospect of personal gain too tempting. The former VP at FCA got greedy and tapped into the UAW-Chrysler NTC fund to buy a car, pay off a student loan, and make expensive home improvements.[37]

Third, personal greed allegedly motivated those at the International's Solidarity House and Region 5.[38] Through accounting schemes, the participating union officials charged large purchases for meals, golfing, and recreational ancillaries to the UAW. They also extracted large amounts of cash for similar purposes. Whether there was motivation to these embezzlement schemes beyond greed is speculation. Clearly, an important question which merits more research is how Gary Jones, the former Region 5 Director, garnered sufficient

Table 1.4 UAW and Corporate Officials Charged with Wrongdoing in Scandal[36]

Person and Position	Conviction	Scandal
Gary Jones, UAW International President and Region 5 Director	June 3, 2020 pled guilty: embezzlement; racketeering; tax fraud 46–57 months/awaiting sentencing	International, Region 5, Palm Springs
Vance Pearson, Region 5 Director	February 7, 2020 pled guilty: embezzlement; racketeering Awaiting sentencing	International, Region 5, Palm Springs
Eugene Robinson, Region 5, UAW Midwest CAP Director	March 2, 2020 pled guilty: embezzlement; defrauding US Awaiting sentencing	International, Region 5, Palm Springs
Joseph Ashton, International UAW VP	December 5, 2019 pled guilty: wire fraud; money laundering Awaiting sentencing	UAW-GM CHR
Michael Grimes, Senior UAW official	September 4, 2019 pled guilty: wire fraud; money laundering 28 months	UAW-GM CHR
Jeffrey Pietrzyck, Senior UAW official	October 22, 2019 pled guilty: wire fraud; money laundering Awaiting sentencing	UAW-GM CHR
Michael Brown, Director, Employee Relations, FCA	May 25, 2018 pled guilty: misprision of a felony 12 months	UAW-Chrysler NTC
Jerome Durden, Financial Analyst, FCA	August 8, 2017 pled guilty: defraud the US; false tax returns 15 months	UAW-Chrysler NTC
Alphons Iacobelli, Vice President, Employee Relations, FCA	July 26, 2017 pled guilty: violation of Labor Management Relations Act (LMRA); defraud US; false tax return 66 months	UAW-Chrysler NTC
Norwood Jewell, International UAW VP	April 2, 2019 pled guilty: violation of LMRA 15 months	UAW-Chrysler NTC
Virdell King, UAW official	August 29, 2017 pled guilty: violation of LMRA 60 days	UAW-Chrysler NTC

(Continued)

Table 1.4 (Cont.)

Person and Position	Conviction	Scandal
Nancy A. Johnson, UAW official	July 23, 2018 pled guilty: violation of LMRA 12 months	UAW-Chrysler NTC
Keith Mickens, UAW official	April 5, 2018 pled guilty: violation of LMRA 12 months	UAW-Chrysler NTC
Monica Morgan, Vendor, spouse of late UAW International VP Holiefield	September 26, 2017 pled guilty: violation of LMRA; defraud US false tax return 18 months	UAW-Chrysler NTC
	IMPLICATED	
General Holiefield, late UAW International VP		UAW-Chrysler NTC
Sergio Marchionne, late CEO, FCA		UAW-Chrysler NTC
Dennis Williams, former International President, UAW		International, Region 5, Palm Springs

support from the Administrative Caucus to win election as UAW International President at the 2018 convention.

The misconduct exhibited by these various UAW and corporate officials clearly violated federal laws. Among the UAW officials, the conduct also breached the union's ethical practices codes, which is embedded in its Constitution since 1957. Since the scandal broke in the news, the UAW, under Presidents Dennis Williams, Gary Jones, and Rory Gamble, has introduced additional financial and operational controls to mitigate the chances of such wrongdoing from recurring. While such "reforms" may be necessary as an additional precaution, they do not address the impure motives of the conspirators; nor do they confront the question of whether there is something intrinsically problematic at the UAW which allowed these overt criminal acts to become so widespread.

We argue that the circumstances which lent themselves to the creation of what the US Attorney's office has labeled a "culture of corruption" and its enabling "culture of alcohol" revolve around the immutable force of bureaucracy blended with one-party dominance that led to a sense of entitlement and complacency.[39] The UAW evolved into a one-caucus-dominated bureaucracy focused on sustaining its administrative and personnel apparatus. The Administrative Caucus became the singular pathway to success and comfort within the union machine and hierarchy.[40]

Specifically, we argue that there was too little accountability and transparency in how the funds allocated to the UAW-Detroit 3 training centers, in two instances, were spent. The management and oversight of the centers appeared lax in the case of UAW-Chrysler NTC and UAW-GM CHR, enabling the misappropriation of substantial amounts of money for personal gain. In the case of the NTC, the motivation behind the bribery of union officials initiated by the highest-ranking corporate officials was to induce corporate-friendly labor-management relations. In this process, the company subsidized union operations through the center.[41] The common thread throughout the three clusters of scandal, supplemented by the UAW-paid embellishes to living quarters at its training facility in Black Lake, was greed, which tempted not only selected union officials but also at least one major corporate figure who had power over labor-management relations.[42]

The Future

The sheer nature and breadth of the scandalous conduct has led to several attempts by three successive presidents to "reform" the UAW, calls for a special constitutional convention, and demands for a government takeover. We address the merits of these proposals in a later chapter. We pay particular attention to the proposal for a government takeover, using the IBT consent decree in 1989 as a point of analytical reference. We hasten to note that a government takeover is not the panacea that some may think.

In short, the UAW today finds itself in the midst of intense criticism and scrutiny. It confronts an aggressive ongoing investigation by several federal agencies coordinated through the US Attorney's office. A government takeover looms in the background. Certainly, there is ample grist for the mill for those within the union's ranks who are pushing grassroots change that would provide for the direct election of members of the IEB. However, we caution that some proposed reforms are not panaceas. A government takeover raises other issues, especially if one uses the "precedent" of the IBT consent decree as a model. The UAW's situation, we submit, is quite different the one that led to the 1989 consent decree in that the IBT was mob infested. No evidence exists that the UAW has had mob connections.

Notes

1 Serrin, *op. cit.*; Stieber, *op.cit.*; Barnard, *op. cit.*
2 Adams, 2010, *op. cit.*
3 Canis et al., *op. cit.*
4 Cutcher-Gershenfeld et al., *op.cit.*
5 Adams, 2010, *op.cit.*
6 Adams, 2019, *op. cit.*; Brooks, 2020, *op. cit.*
7 Mickens, Plea Bargain, *op. cit.*; Iacobelli, Plea Bargain, *op. cit.*; Iacobelli, Indictment, *op. cit.* GM Civil RICO Complaint, *op. cit.*; GM Amended Civil Complaint, *op. cit.*

8 Iacobelli, Indictment; Plea Bargain; Confessions; *op. cit.* GM Civil RICO Complaint, *op. cit.*; GM Amended RIOC Complaint, *op. cit.*; US Attorney (June 3, 2020), *op cit.*
9 GM Civil RICO Complaint, *op. cit.*
10 GM Amended Civil Complaint, *op. cit.*
11 Grimes, Plea Bargain, *op. cit.*; Ashton, Plea Bargain, *op. cit.*; Pietryzk, Plea Bargain, *op. cit.*
12 GM Amended Civil Complaint, *op. cit.*; Brown, Plea Bargain, *op. cit.*; Mickens, Plea Bargain, *op. cit.*
13 Reuther, *op. cit.* Serrin, *op. cit.*; Barnard, *op. cit.*; Stieber, *op. cit.*; Adams, 2010, *op. cit.*
14 Serrin, *op. cit.*
15 Adams, 2010, *op. cit.*, Barnard, *op. cit.*, Serrin, *op. cit.*, Stieber, *op. cit.*, Reuther, *op. cit.*, Ford Motor Company (2015), 2015 *UAW-Ford: National Negotiations Media Fact Book*; http://www.uaw.org
16 Serrin, *op. cit.*, p. 129.
17 Baime, A.J. (2014). *The Arsenal of Democracy: FDR, Detroit, and an Epic Quest to Arm an America at War.* Boston: Houghton Mifflin Harcourt.
18 Barnard, *op. cit.*; Serrin, *op. cit.*; Stieber, *op. cit.*; Reuther, *op. cit.*; http://www.cargroup.org/wp-content/uploads/2017/02/2011-Detroit-3_UAW-Labor-Contract-Negotiations.pdf; https://uaw.org/see-summary-tentative-agreement-gm/; https://uaw.org/wp-content/uploads/2019/12/56461-UAW-Hourly_rev3.pdf; https://uaw.org/uaw-auto-bargaining/fordcontract/; https://uaw.org/uaw-auto-bargaining/fca-us/; https://uaw.org/wp-content/uploads/2015/11/reducedFINAL-FORD-HOURLY-11-9-15-1229p-FINAL-with-numbers-p24-headings-page-6-charts-p25.pdf; https://uaw.org/contractsummary/; https://uaw.org/fordhighlighter/; https://uaw.org/uaw-auto-bargaining/; Ford Motor Company, 2015, *op. cit.*; Ford Motor Company (2019). *2019 UAW-Ford: National Negotiations Media Fact Book. 2015 UAW-Ford: National Negotiations Media Fact Book.*
19 Shermer, E.T. (2008). Origins of the Conservative Ascendancy: Barry Goldwater's Early Senate Career and the De-legitimization of Organized Labor, *Journal of American History*, 94 (December): 701.
20 Estey et al., *op. cit.*
21 Stieber, *op. cit.*; Serrin, *op. cit.*
22 Howes, D. and Snell, R. (2019, December 18). Driven by Greed: Alliance of FCA, Union Leaders Fueled Decade of Corruption, *The Detroit News*.
23 Scott, R.E. (2003). *NAFTA-Related Job Losses Have Piled Up,* Economic Policy Institute, December 10, 2003.
24 Adams, 2010, *op. cit.*; Cutcher-Gershenfeld et al., *op. cit.*
25 Bickley, *op. cit.*
26 Canis et al., *op. cit.*
27 Cooney, *op. cit.*; Canis and Yacubucci, *op. cit.*
28 Spero, S.D. (1948). *Government as Employer.* Carbondale, IL: Southern Illinois University Press; Hart, W.R. (1961). *Collective Bargaining in the Federal Civil Service.* New York: Harper & Brothers Publishers.
29 Burden and Snell, *op. cit.*
30 Ibid.
31 GM Civil RICO Complaint, *op. cit.*; GM Amended Civil Complaint, *op. cit.*; Iacobelli, Indictment; *op. cit.*; Brown, Plea Bargain, *op. cit.*; Mickens, Plea Bargain, *op. cit.*
32 Ibid.
33 Iacobelli, Sentencing Hearing, *op. cit.*

34 Adams, 2010, *op. cit*; Adams 2019, *op. cit.*
35 Howes and Snell, 2019, *op. cit.*
36 Iacobelli, Sentencing Memorandum, *op. cit.*; Iacobelli, Indictment, *op. cit.*; GM Civil RICO Complaint, *op. cit.*; Ashton, Criminal Complaint, *op. cit.*; Ashton, Plea Bargain, *op. cit.*; Grimes, Plea Bargain, *op. cit.*; GM Civil RICO Complaint, *op. cit.*; GM Amended Civil Complaint, *op. cit.*; Pietrzyk, Plea Bargain, *op. cit.*; Mickens, Plea Bargain, *op. cit.*; Iacobelli, Indictment, *op. cit.*; Ashton, Sentencing Memorandum, *op. cit.*; Iacobelli, Confessions, *op. cit.*; Durden, Plea Bargain, *op. cit.*; Nancy Johnson, Plea Bargain, *op. cit.*; Robinson, Criminal Complaint, *op. cit.*; Jones, Criminal Complaint, *op. cit.*; Jones, Plea Bargain, *op. cit.*, Pearson, Criminal Complaint, *op. cit.*; Jewell, Plea Bargain, *op. cit.*; Virdell King, Plea Bargain, *op. cit.*
37 Ibid.
38 Mickens, Plea Bargain, *op. cit.*; GM Civil RICO Complaint, *op. cit.*; GM Amended Civil Complaint, *op. cit.*
39 Adams, 2010, *op. cit.*; 2019, *op. cit.*
40 Mickens, Plea Bargain, *op. cit.*; Brown, Plea Bargain, *op. cit.*; Iacobelli, Indictment; Plea Bargain; Sentencing Memorandum; Confessions, *op. cit.*; GM Civil RIOC Complaint, *op. cit.*; GM Amended Civil Complaint, *op. cit.*
41 Ibid.
42 Ibid.

Chapter 2

The UAW

Governance, Membership, and Organization

The United Auto Workers is officially titled the International Union, United Automobile, Aerospace, and Agricultural Implement Workers of America (UAW). Established in 1935, it held its first convention in 1936, with about 30,000 members.[1] The UAW's Constitution and Bylaws govern the organization and delineate the powers of the governing bodies, procedures for electing officers, and the rights and responsibilities of union members and officers.[2] Its Constitution also defines its industrial jurisdiction and criteria for admitting members and determining eligibility to vote in various internal elections. As a labor organization, the UAW must abide by various federal and state laws which impose reporting requirements and legal standards governing its conduct and the conduct of its officers. These include filing annual financial disclosure reports with the US Department of Labor (DOL). The UAW has a constitutionally established procedure for appealing its decisions (the Public Review Board) and an Ethical Practices Codes of Conduct, violations of which may warrant the expulsion of union officers. We review various aspects of the nature and operation of the UAW, discussing relevant constitutional provisions. In so doing, we provide a current snapshot of the union as an organization.

Governance

The supreme governing authority of the UAW is its convention. The regular convention meets quadrennially to elect officers and establish policies. At this convocation, the elected delegates choose the members of the International Executive Board (IEB), which is the governing body in between conventions. It currently consists of 13 members: five international officers and eight regional directors. The UAW's IEB voted in December 2019 to merge Region 5, which included 17 western and southwestern states, into Regions 4 and 8, effective February 28, 2020.[3] The regions represent different geographies within which UAW members are found. The "top" officers of the union are the International President, International Secretary-Treasurer, and three International Vice Presidents. [Given its current bargaining structure, the

International Vice Presidents are associated with three departments aligned with the three major auto-manufacturing companies operating in the US: Ford, GM, and Fiat Chrysler Automobiles, FCA (which, as noted, is on a path to merging with the PSA Group, a French-based conglomerate, to be renamed Stellantis in 2021)].[4] The IEB is empowered to authorize strikes, issue charters, and discipline subordinate bodies for violating the UAW Constitution. On the day-to-day basis, the chief authority in the union is the International President, who is responsible for executing the instructions of the IEB and administering the UAW.

The election of the members of the IEB is heavily influenced by the so-called Administrative Caucus (hereinafter referred to as the Caucus), whose origin dates to the 1940s when the venerated Walter Reuther assumed the UAW presidency and began to consolidate power among vying internal factions.[5] Originally known as the Reuther Caucus, the Administrative Caucus nominates UAW members for office, including positions on the IEB. The current membership of the IEB recommends a slate of candidates for the board, which is considered by a larger body of the Caucus. The Caucus typically approves these recommendations and forwards them to the convention delegates, who in turn vote on the candidates vying for position. Generally speaking, the Caucus-endorsed candidates win, though there have been a few occasions in which dissidents have been elected to office.

The convention consists of delegates elected by the membership by secret ballot from the various affiliated units. Each local union may elect one delegate for its first 200 members, a second for an additional 300 members, and one more for each additional 800 members. Each local union is entitled to one convention vote for its first 100 members and one additional vote for each additional 100 members. No delegate to a convention may have more than eight votes. It takes 25 percent of the delegates to constitute a quorum. The Constitution provides for the convening of a special convention by instruction of the IEB or a referendum if a sufficient number of rank-and-file across a minimum number of local unions so petition. Parenthetically, this latter option has been invoked recently by a dissident group with the UAW, the Unite All Workers for Democracy (UAWD), which is petitioning for special convention to enact changes in the election of members of the IEB.[6]

Within the UAW organizational structure, there are several types of affiliated units. The most populous are *local unions* [approximately 600 in number], which are established by a constitutional procedure requiring that at least 15 persons working under the jurisdiction of the International Union apply to the International Secretary-Treasurer for a charter. [Each chartered local union is required to elect a president, vice president, financial secretary, three trustees, a recording secretary, Sergeant-at-Arms, and Guide. Elections are held by secret ballot among eligible members of the local union.] A second category of units is the *amalgamated local union*, which consists of two or more locals within the geography of region. In addition, a region may establish a *District Council* to make recommendations to the regional director on improving the welfare of its membership. Forming a District Council requires a majority of the local unions in a region representing a majority of the regional membership.

The Constitution specifies several departments to be part of the International's operations, which are headquartered at Solidarity House located on 8000 East Jefferson Avenue, Detroit, MI 48214 [the headquarters has temporarily moved to a rented building in Southfield, MI due to a July 2019 fire at 8000 East Jefferson Ave]. They include: Civil and Human Rights, Education, Research, Communications, Competitive Shops, and the Family Education Center. There is also constitutional provision for the establishment of Community Action Program (CAP) Councils, including a National Community Action Program Council. The CAPs are charged with promoting policies and programs to improve and enrich American life. They serve essentially as political action committees (PACs), which, under federal election laws, raise money from union members and their families on a strictly voluntary basis.[7] Union PAC money, in turn, may be contributed to candidates for federal office, within prescribed limits under federal election campaign laws.

The UAW includes several noteworthy features aimed at ensuring that it operates democratically and ethically. First, in 1957, it created a seven-member Public Review Board (PRB), later reduced to four members, with each member appointed from outside the UAW to be independent.[8] The PRB hears appeals of decisions made by various authorities within the union. It also deals with alleged violations any of the UAW Ethical Practices Codes, which is the second feature. The Codes includes four main parts: Democratic Practices; Financial Practices; Health, Welfare, and Retirement Funds; and Business and Financial Activities of Union Officials. The Democratic Practices clause espouses several principles, including members' rights to: freedom of speech; run for union office; criticize the Union and its leaders; participate freely in union meetings and elections; appeal adverse decisions; maintain a corruption-free union; and the fair application of union rules and laws. The provision on Democratic Practices specifically states in part that:

> Each member shall be entitled to a full share in Union self-government. Each member shall have full freedom of speech and the right to participate in the democratic decisions of the Union. Subject to reasonable rules and regulations, each member shall have the right to run for office, to nominate and to vote in free, fair and honest elections. In a democratic union, as in a democratic society, every member has certain rights but s/he also must accept certain corresponding obligations.[9]

The Codes on Financial Practices entitles members to the: proper use and investment of union funds; competitive bidding for major contracts; and protection against the use of funds for personal gain of officers and representatives of the union. More specifically, the Codes stipulate that:

> Union funds are held in sacred trust for the benefit of the membership. The membership is entitled to assurance that Union funds are not dissipated and are spent for proper purposes. The membership is also entitled to be reasonably informed as to how Union funds are invested or used.[10]

The section of the Codes dealing with the business and financial activities of union officials states that:

> No officer or representative shall accept "kickbacks," under-the-table payments, valuable gifts, lavish entertainment or any personal payment of any kind, other than regular pay and benefits for work performed as an employee from an employer with which the Union bargains or from a business or professional enterprise with which the Union does business. The principles of this Code, of course, apply to investments.[11]

In sum, these Codes provide unambiguous guidance about what is acceptable versus unacceptable conduct in these sensitive areas. Any union official who reads the Ethical Practices Codes with an intent to abide by its various provisions knows beyond any doubt that the conduct which occurred across the UAW scandal represented a clear breach of ethics.

Structure

The nominal structure of the UAW represents a pyramid. Membership lies at the base of the pyramid. Rank-and-file combine to form local unions, which are the organizational layer closest to the rank-and-file. Amalgamated local unions and District Councils represent joint operations among locals. The top layers of pyramid include the various members of the International Executive Board: eight Regional Directors; three International Vice Presidents; the International Secretary-Treasurer; and the International President. An intermediate type of organization is the Community Action Program (CAP) Council, of which there are 11 in the UAW, including the National CAP Council.

Approximately 84 percent of the UAW's 2018 members are affiliated with the 210 locals that file LM-2 financial disclosure forms with the US Department of Labor (DOL). Roughly one-third of the UAW membership belongs to the largest 20 locals. [We will report more details about the locals, as well as the CAP Councils, later in this chapter.]

We report here on the nine former regions of the UAW in existence at the time the scandal occurred and was investigated by the US Attorney's office. The nine districts cover the US and Canada (see Table 2.1). Regions 1, 1A, and 1D are located in Michigan and Canada. Region 2B represents Indiana

Table 2.1 Geographical Breakdown of UAW Regions[12]

Region	States and Other Locations
1	Canada and eight counties in Michigan: Huron, Lapeer, Macomb, Oakland, St. Clair, Sanilac, Tuscola, and Wayne (partial)
1A	Three counties in Michigan: Monroe, Washtenaw, and Wayne (partial)
1D	The Upper Peninsula of Michigan; the central, western, and northern portions of the Lower Peninsula of Michigan
2B	Ohio and Indiana
4	Illinois, Iowa, Nebraska, Wisconsin, Minnesota, North Dakota, Wyoming, and Montana
5	Missouri, Arkansas, Oklahoma, Louisiana, Kansas, Texas, Colorado, New Mexico, Washington, Oregon, California, Idaho, Alaska, Nevada, Utah, Arizona, Alaska, and Hawaii
8	Tennessee, Virginia, West Virginia, North Carolina, South Carolina, Mississippi, Alabama, Georgia, District of Columbia, Maryland, Delaware, Kentucky, Florida, and Pennsylvania (four counties)
9	West and Central New York, New Jersey, and Pennsylvania (remaining)
9A	Eastern New York (including New York City and metropolitan area, Hudson Valley, and Capital District areas), Connecticut, Massachusetts, Rhode Island, New Hampshire, Vermont, Maine, and Puerto Rico

Source: UAW

Note: Effective February 28, 2020, Region 5 was split and Kansas, Missouri, Oregon, Washington, Idaho, Nevada, Alaska and Hawaii were moved to Region 4. Arkansas, Texas, Louisiana, New Mexico, Arizona, Colorado, Oklahoma, Utah and California were moved to Region 8.

and Ohio. Nine states are included in Region 4, including Illinois, Iowa, Wisconsin, Wyoming, and Montana. Region 5 formerly spanned 17 states west of the Mississippi, and was split in February 2020 and merged with Regions 4 and 8. Region 8 includes the Southern states, District of Columbia, and four counties of Pennsylvania. Mid-Atlantic and Northern Eastern/New England states fall under Regions 9 and 9A.

Membership

Members of the UAW have certain privileges and responsibilities. Members can attend local meetings, vote for local officers and International Convention delegates, and vote in strike authorizations and contract ratifications. Members also have the right to inspect the verbatim minutes of IEB meetings at the office of the International Secretary-Treasurer or Regional District office (although very few members exercise this right). To be a member in good standing, a worker must keep dues payments up to date. Members who retire are not required to pay dues, but retain all of the privileges of membership except for strike votes, contract ratification votes, and votes for elected shop floor representatives.

The UAW Constitution defines its jurisdiction broadly, encompassing workers in the automobile, aerospace, and agricultural implements industries, as well as employees engaged in various occupations in the broader private and public sectors, including workers in gaming establishments. The specific language of its jurisdiction merits note to capture the full scope of eligibility:

> The International Union, United Automobile, Aerospace and Agricultural Implement Workers of America (UAW), shall take in and hold jurisdiction over all employees in workplaces engaged in the manufacture of parts (including tools, dies, etc.), and the assembly of these parts into farm, automobile, automotive propelled products, aerospace and agricultural implements, including employees engaged in office work, sales, distribution and maintenance thereof. Its jurisdiction shall also encompass service, technical, office and/ or professional workplaces, whether public or private, and gaming establishments and others as the International Executive Board shall decide. The jurisdiction of this International Union shall be full and final.[13]

To be eligible for union membership, a worker must apply to a local union having jurisdiction over the workplace in which the person is employed. According to Article 6 of the Constitution, "The applicant must, at the time of application, be an actual worker in and around the workplace."

The UAW's membership has fluctuated dramatically over time. It grew from a nucleus of about 30,000 in the mid-1930s, at the time of its initial formation, to more than 1.2 million in 1959 (see Table 2.2). Membership peaked at over 1.5 million in 1979. It had fallen to just above 670,000 by 2000. After the Great Recession, its membership had dropped to under 377,000 in 2010, before rising to 408,639 by 2015. In 2018, the UAW's membership stood at 395,703, having dropped by about 36,000 from the previous year. In 2019, despite the news of the scandals being made public, the UAW gained an additional 3,126 members.

Dues and Salaries

The UAW convention delegates determine the dues rates paid by members and the salaries paid to members of the International Executive Board, which are pegged to the salary set for International Representatives. Hourly workers dues are set currently at two hours of pay per month if the UAW's strike fund is at $850 million or above; salaried workers pay 0.805 percent of their monthly gross salary (Table 2.3). If the strike fund is between $650 and $850 million, hourly workers pay 2.5 hours of monthly wages; salaried workers pay 1.15 percent of their monthly gross salaries. Public sector workers who are forbidden by law to strike, and thus cannot avail themselves of the benefits of the strike fund, pay a slightly lower rate of dues.

Table 2.2 UAW Membership, Selected Years 1959–2019[14]

Year	Members
1959	1,124,362
1969	1,530,870
1979	1,527,858
1993	750,436
2000	671,853
2005	557,099
2010	376,612
2015	408,639
2017	430,871
2018	395,703
2019	398,829

Source: UAW

Note: Membership decreased 73.9% from 1979 to 2019

Table 2.3 UAW Member Monthly Dues Rates[15]

		Sector	
Size of UAW Strike and Defense Fund	Classification	With Legal Right To Strike	Without Legal Right To Strike
$850 million and greater	Hourly, ≥ 40 hours/month	2 hours	1.4 hours
	Salaried, and Non-Traditional Sector Part-Time Hourly	1.15%	0.805%
$650 to $850 million	Hourly, ≥ 40 hours/month	2.5 hours	1.9 hours
	Salaried, and Non-Traditional Sector Part-Time Hourly	1.44%	1.095%

Source: UAW Constitution, 2018

Note: Hourly dues rates are based on the hourly straight time pay rate multiplied by the above dues rate. Salary dues rates are based upon straight time monthly wages. Public sector workers who are prohibited by law from striking pay lower dues rates because they do not contribute to the strike fund.

The UAW Constitution pegs the pay of the IEB to the salary the convention sets for International Representatives (see Table 2.4). Based on the 2018 convention, International Representatives earn salaries of $114,476.15. The International President's pay is set at 1.8 times the International Representative salary; Secretary-Treasurer at 1.67 times; International Vice Presidents at 1.62; and Regional Directors are paid 1.49 times the International Representative.

UAW Locals and CAP Councils

The UAW is a nominally decentralized institution. Workers join the UAW at the local level. As noted, the UAW has more than 600 locals scattered across the United States and Canada. They represent a wide variety of industries and occupations, from auto workers and nurses to graduate students and gaming workers. In 2018, there were 210 local unions filing LM-2 financial disclosure forms with the US Department of Labor under the LMRDA. [Labor organizations with annual receipts at or above $250,000 file the LM-2 form, which is more detailed than the LM-3 form which applies to organizations with less than $250,000 in annual receipts; labor organizations with less than $10,000 in annual receipts file an even simpler LM-4.] These 210 locals represented 332,306 employees. In 2018, they had a total of nearly $235 million in net assets and collected close to $272.3 million in revenues, of which they spent almost $267 million. As shown in Table 2.5, the 20 largest UAW locals had memberships that ranged from 3,755 (UAW Local 974) to 22,803 (Local 600). Seven of the 20 locals are headquartered in Michigan. The combined membership of the top 20 is 130,808, and they had net assets of nearly $75 million.

The UAW has approximately 78 CAP organizations, 11 of which file LM-2s. The CAP Councils are essentially political organizations which attempt to influence elections at all levels of government. They must comply with various federal and state election campaign financing laws, such as the Federal Election Campaign Act of 1971, as amended. As shown in Table 2.6, the 11 Councils, which include the UAW's National CAP, had $6.9 million in total assets in

Table 2.4 UAW International Executive Board Annual Salaries[16]

International Representative (IR)	*$111,476.15*
President	1.8 Times IR Salary
Secretary-Treasurer	1.67 Times IR Salary
Vice Presidents	1.62 Times IR Salary
IEB Members (Regional Directors)	1.49 Times IR Salary

Source: UAW Constitution, 2018

Note: International Representatives and International Executive Board members are also eligible to receive lump sum payments of up to 3%-4% of salaries if the membership in the industrial sectors receive profit sharing payments.

Table 2.5 Financial Information for the 20 Largest UAW Locals by Membership, 2018[17]

Local	State	Net Assets	Assets	Liabilities	Receipts	Disbursements	Members
600	MI	$ 4,045,128	$ 5,033,170	$ 988,042	$ 11,637,587	$ 11,311,057	22,803
862	KY	$ 8,765,905	$ 9,295,023	$ 529,118	$ 11,992,175	$ 11,367,123	13,498
12	OH	$ 6,343,238	$ 6,712,628	$ 369,390	$ 6,804,347	$ 6,154,576	9,401
249	MO	$ 8,074,822	$ 8,466,516	$ 391,694	$ 7,223,015	$ 6,901,204	9,227
72	WI	$ 1,796,030	$ 1,797,135	$ 1,105	$ 171,568	$ 275,597	7,722
1700	MI	$ 2,042,585	$ 2,372,202	$ 329,617	$ 5,315,889	$ 4,216,254	7,493
685	IN	$ 6,299,460	$ 6,626,287	$ 326,827	$ 6,076,894	$ 6,295,255	6,302
1268	IL	$ 4,154,282	$ 4,451,307	$ 297,025	$ 5,455,039	$ 4,921,559	5,886
155	MI	$ 2,470,955	$ 2,582,333	$ 111,378	$ 3,124,215	$ 3,435,222	5,208
7	MI	$ 4,436,078	$ 4,698,055	$ 261,977	$ 4,375,913	$ 4,063,993	4,681
140	MI	$ 2,426,417	$ 2,439,736	$ 13,319	$ 3,115,520	$ 3,092,307	4,595
551	IL	$ 1,027,012	$ 1,225,791	$ 198,779	$ 4,033,087	$ 4,059,366	4,580
2209	IN	$ 2,623,683	$ 2,625,439	$ 1,756	$ 4,381,928	$ 4,239,148	4,538
900	MI	$ 4,766,665	$ 4,939,753	$ 173,088	$ 3,293,755	$ 3,632,099	4,316
2320	NY	$ 2,111,027	$ 2,116,841	$ 5,814	$ 3,690,647	$ 3,625,912	4,314
3000	MI	$ 1,920,677	$ 2,198,335	$ 277,658	$ 3,662,200	$ 3,688,891	4,276
1853	TN	$ 8,316,085	$ 8,484,746	$ 168,661	$ 3,894,440	$ 4,027,986	4,253
2250	MO	$ 2,145,937	$ 2,356,587	$ 210,650	$ 3,644,662	$ 3,510,758	3,960
974	IL	$ 989,608	$ 1,144,522	$ 154,914	$ 2,599,863	$ 2,426,486	3,755
276	TX	$ 1,304,374	$ 1,520,123	$ 215,749	$ 3,933,710	$ 4,004,319	3,680
Total		$ 76,059,968	$ 81,086,529	$ 5,026,561	$ 98,426,454	$ 95,249,112	134,488

Source: US Department of Labor 2018 LM-2 Reports
Note: Net Assets = Assets minus Liabilities

Table 2.6 UAW CAP Councils with more than $250,000 in receipts, 2018[18]

CAP Location		Name	Assets	Receipts	Disbursements	Members
Detroit	MI	National CAP	$ 710,884	$ 4,544,800	$ 4,059,694	395,703
Detroit	MI	Michigan CAP	$ 160,351	$ 1,700,956	$ 1,998,975	141,522
Maumee	OH	Auto Workers AFL-CIO CAP Council	$ 1,447,296	$ 765,959	$ 691,278	43,929
Lincolnshire	IL	Illinois State Cap	$ 146,048	$ 761,679	$ 740,753	26,941
Detroit	MI	Region 1 CAP	$ 1,081,585	$ 564,987	$ 631,328	53,414
Lebanon	TN	Region 8 CAP	$ 39,006	$ 512,186	$ 534,126	40,533
Dallas	TX	Southwestern States CAP - Region 5	$ 787,973	$ 465,791	$ 439,247	13,000
Maumee	OH	Auto Workers AFL-CIO CAP Council	$ 1,953,677	$ 436,866	$ 311,990	23,030
Detroit	MI	Region 1-D CAP	$ 427,919	$ 379,042	$ 548,900	45,413
Detroit	MI	Region 1-A CAP	$ 16,626	$ 359,784	$ 408,919	42,695
Hazelwood	MO	CAP Council - Region 5 Midwest States	$ 177,703	$ 301,148	$ 313,560	8,850
Total			$ 6,949,068	$ 10,793,198	$10,678,770	

Notes: Total UAW CAP Receipts, including 67 smaller CAP Councils, is $13,215,454 in 2018. Membership may overlap CAP Councils

2018 and generated almost $10.8 million in revenue. The National CAP collected over 40 percent of the total receipts (roughly $4.5 million).

UAW Officers and Employees

In 2018, the UAW reported having 685 employees for which it paid gross salaries, including allowances and reimbursements for expenses, totaling $71,648,681. There were 431 employees among this group who were paid more than $100,000 in gross income in that year. The highest paid employee grossed $182,598. The UAW also reported having paid salaries for 21 international officers, some of whom were paid for only part of the year. Of these, 20 earned more than $100,000 in gross income. The highest paid was International President Gary Jones, whose gross income, including allowances and expenses, totaled $260,243. On average, the officers spent over 84 percent of their time on representational activities and less than six percent on political action. The paid employees spent about 83 percent on representational activities and less than five percent on political action.

Notes

1 Serrin, *op. cit.*; Adams, 2010, *op. cit.*; Barnard, *op. cit.*
2 United Auto Workers (2020). *Constitution of the International Union*, https://ua w.org/uaw-constitution-2/.
3 Thibodeau, I., and Howes, D. (2019, December 6). UAW Moving to Disband Region 5 Embroiled in Federal Probe, *Detroit Free Press.*
4 Wall-Howard, *op. cit.*
5 Stieber, *op. cit.*
6 Lawrence, E.D. (2020, January 24). UAW Reformers Want to Change How Leaders Are Picked, *Detroit Free Press.*
7 Congressional Research Service, *op. cit.*
8 Stieber, *op. cit.*; Ewing, L. (2005). *Ethical Practices in a Labor Union: The Case of the UAW,* in J. Budd and J. Scoville (Eds.), *The Ethics of Human Resources and Industrial Relations,* Champaign, IL: Labor and Employment Relations Association.
9 United Auto Workers, Constitution, *op. cit.*
10 Ibid.
11 Ibid.
12 Thibodeau and Howes, *op. cit.*; UAW News Release, February 28, 2020: https:// uaw.org/uaw-merges-additional-states-region-8-region-4//
13 United Auto Workers, Constitution, *op. cit.*
14 Masters, *op. cit.*; Adams, 2010, *op. cit.*; UAW LM-2 forms filed with US DOL, OLMS.
15 United Auto Workers, Constitution, *op. cit.*
16 Ibid.
17 UAW LM-2 forms filed with US DOL, OLMS.
18 Ibid.

Chapter 3

UAW Finances

The scandal that engulfed the UAW revolved around the illegal and problematic use of money. Participants tapped three sources for the money to commit bribery, embezzlement, fraud, extortion, and the corrupting of the integrity of labor-management relations: (1) the joint training programs; (2) the UAW's general treasury; and (3) selected CAPs. We gathered data on the UAW's finances from annual LM-2 disclosure forms filed with the US Department of Labor, which are available online through a portal managed by the DOL's Office of Labor-Management Standards (OLMS, an entity which collects and discloses data on union finances and investigates evidence of wrongdoing under relevant labor law).

In this chapter, we review the financial state of the UAW itself, focusing on its balance sheets and income statements, covering selected years between 2000 and 2018 (which the latest year for which data are available at the time of this writing; the US DOL had granted unions an extension to file the 2019 forms due to the pandemic; the UAW filed its 2019 form in late June 2020). More specifically, we report on the UAW's overall financial wealth and its disbursements and receipts. We break down assets, liabilities, receipts, and disbursements by major categories and report more detail on the compensation of officers and employees of the union. Our data also cover the UAW's revenue from member-based income (MBI), which includes per capita taxes, dues, and fees, plus its operating budget. We report the ratio of its operating budget to MBI to show the UAW's relative capacity to finance ongoing operations from revenues generated by the membership. The changing financial state of the union has implications for understanding the motivation behind the push to tap into the funds of the joint training centers to subsidize the UAW International's operating budget.

UAW Wealth, Income, and Disbursements

Table 3.1 reveals the UAW's total assets, net assets, receipts, and disbursements over the years from 2000 to 2018. The union's total assets have ranged from $944 million to almost $1.268 billion. From the peak year of 2006, the UAW's

Table 3.1 UAW Assets, Liabilities, Receipts, Disbursements (in thousands): 2000–2018[1]

Year	Assets	Liabilities	Net Assets	Receipts	Disbursements
2018	$ 1,120,820	$ 115,925	$ 1,004,895	$ 256,383	$ 258,264
2017	$ 1,069,381	$ 122,177	$ 947,204	$ 273,613	$ 272,055
2016	$ 997,325	$ 135,623	$ 861,702	$ 261,207	$ 263,149
2015	$ 944,968	$ 9,349	$ 935,619	$ 289,117	$ 288,023
2014	$ 978,107	$ 6,589	$ 971,519	$ 219,808	$ 218,799
2013	$ 989,948	$ 7,380	$ 982,568	$ 214,010	$ 213,990
2012	$ 1,003,949	$ 7,698	$ 996,252	$ 261,144	$ 260,201
2011	$ 1,043,684	$ 7,137	$ 1,036,547	$ 257,779	$ 258,115
2010	$ 1,077,324	$ 4,590	$ 1,072,734	$ 274,044	$ 275,068
2009	$ 1,130,127	$ 5,605	$ 1,124,523	$ 277,402	$ 279,482
2008	$ 1,199,623	$ 5,773	$ 1,193,851	$ 315,772	$ 310,115
2007	$ 1,251,687	$ 5,543	$ 1,246,144	$ 327,638	$ 330,339
2006	$ 1,267,560	$ 35,459	$ 1,232,101	$ 303,825	$ 304,925
2005	$ 1,235,804	$ 3,879	$ 1,231,925	$ 306,748	$ 306,098
2004	$ 1,188,106	$ 3,060	$ 1,185,046	$ 325,668	$ 322,136
2003	$ 1,136,188	$ 2,851	$ 1,133,337	$ 325,079	$ 327,360
2002	$ 1,146,480	$ 3,413	$ 1,143,067	$ 314,478	$ 316,162
2001	$ 1,142,081	$ 4,287	$ 1,137,794	$ 328,748	$ 327,126
2000	$ 1,100,482	$ 4,967	$ 1,095,514	$ 330,124	$ 331,445

Source: US Department of Labor LM-2 Reports, 2000–2018

overall wealth had declined by roughly 25 percent in 2015. Although its total assets have risen in recent years, the UAW's wealth has still not reached its levels during the 2001 through 2009 years. A similar pattern emerged with net assets, which fell by about 31 percent from a peak during this period in 2007 of almost $1.25 billion to less than $862 million in 2016.

The UAW's total receipts, from all revenue sources, including its per capita tax (or dues equivalent), also fell sharply during this period. Specifically, they dropped from slightly over $330 million in 2000 to just $214 million in 2013, or over 35 percent. Receipts rose significantly in 2015, partly because of the aforementioned dues hike made by the UAW at its 2014 convention. In 2018, total receipts lagged the amount generated in 2000 by more than $60 million. Thus, in nominal dollars, the UAW has significantly less money to spend than it did 20 years ago. As will become evident later, the financial difficulties the UAW experienced in the Great Recession and immediately thereafter threated the union's capacity to service members, necessitating a substantial reduction in union personnel.

Revenues and Disbursements

Table 3.2 reports the UAW's net revenues and disbursements. The net figures subtract the revenues collected for transfer to affiliates and transmittal to members from the total receipts and disbursements. These specific revenues are intra-union exchanges that are not available for general expenditures and thus are subtracted to provide a more accurate indicator of the actual amount the International UAW has available to spend representing members.

The data on net receipts and disbursements reveal patterns similar to the overall totals. The relevant point is that after deducting intra-union exchanges the UAW has a nontrivial amount less to spend. It is the net revenues which actually constrain the real expenditures a union can make. This is the baseline that makes more sense to measure the union's relative spending priorities, to which we turn below.

Table 3.2 UAW Net Revenue, Member-Based Income (MBI), Net Disbursements, Operating Budget (in thousands)[2]

Year	Net Revenue	MBI	Net Disbursements	Operating Budget
2018	$242,313	$180,698	$243,815	$135,098
2017	$259,717	$175,761	$259,937	$129,179
2016	$246,508	$182,485	$247,520	$127,045
2015	$275,559	$168,335	$275,511	$118,890
2014	$206,239	$116,785	$204,654	$129,102
2013	$201,508	$115,110	$201,354	$127,458
2012	$248,204	$114,997	$248,976	$132,928
2011	$245,965	$122,377	$245,943	$141,176
2010	$262,588	$119,017	$262,296	$144,170
2009	$266,212	$127,494	$268,954	$161,464
2008	$303,996	$161,343	$298,545	$170,783
2007	$315,633	$168,793	$317,911	$169,910
2006	$290,610	$191,219	$291,283	$174,144
2005	$293,055	$197,066	$293,599	$165,700
2004	$314,994	$206,489	$291,378	
2003	$316,627	$214,337	$299,111	
2002	$306,894	$209,118	$288,812	
2001	$321,310	$217,377	$301,248	
2000	$323,315	$223,141	$306,341	

Source: US Department of Labor LM-2 Reports

Table 3.2 also reports the UAW's member-based income (MBI, as defined above) and its operating budget for the years between 2000 and 2018 (except in the case of the operating budget for the years between 2000 and 2005, when the format of the reporting form was different and did not include the same items). [Operating budget includes expenditures on representation, general overhead, union administration, and purchases of supplies.] The UAW's MBI declined from a peak during this period of over $223 million in 2000 to a low in 2012 of below $115 million, which is a 48.5 percent drop. Its operating budget was also significantly reduced (31.8 percent) between 2006 and a low in 2015.

Major Categories of Assets and Liabilities

We break down the UAW's assets into four major categories: current assets, non-fixed investments, fixed investments, and other. We show percentage of each category as a share of total assets. Current assets include cash, accounts receivable, and US Treasury Securities, each of which is highly liquid. Non-fixed investments include equities and other non-Treasury bonds. Table 3.3 itemizes the assets held in each category and their percentages of total assets for selected years between 2007 and 2018.

The data reveal a major shift in the composition of asset holdings during this interval. In 2007, almost 60 percent of the assets were current assets, the overwhelming amount of which were held in US Treasuries. Thereafter, the UAW transferred most of its US Treasury securities into equity or non-Treasury bonds. In 2011, only slightly more than seven percent of the total assets were in the current-asset category. Seventy-five percent were held in investments. Across the 11 years reported in Table 3.3 anywhere from 8.2 to 10.4 percent are held in fixed investments. In each of these years, over 79 percent of the assets were held in the investment and current-asset categories. Roughly eight to ten percent were held in fixed investments. During this period, the UAW shifted the bulk of its assets from US Treasury Securities to other types of longer-term investments, such as equities.

Breakdown of Receipts and Disbursements

Tables 3.4 and 3.5 break down the UAW's receipts and disbursements by major categories for selected years between 2007 and 2018. The major categories of receipts are MBI, business income (which includes income from sales of supplies, rents, and dividends), investment income (from the sale of assets and interest on investments), transfers and transmittals (as previously defined), and the catchall category.

As shown in Table 3.4, nearly half to slightly over 70 percent of the UAW's net revenues came from MBI (collected as per capita taxes on members). The second largest category in the years 2007 through 2015 (the

Table 3.3 Major Categories of UAW Assets (in thousands)[3]

Asset Class	2018 Amount	2018 % of Total	2015 Amount	2015 % of Total	2011 Amount	2011 % of Total	2007 Amount	2007 % of Total
Total Assets	$ 1,120,820		$ 944,968		$ 1,043,684		$ 1,251,687	
Investments	$ 711,851	63.51%	$ 650,843	68.87%	$ 782,771	75.00%	$ 360,377	28.79%
Current Assets	$ 201,702	18.00%	$ 100,562	10.64%	$ 75,505	7.23%	$ 732,253	58.50%
Fixed Assets	$ 100,099	8.93%	$ 95,896	10.15%	$ 108,566	10.40%	$ 103,380	8.26%
Loans Receivable	$ 75,377	6.73%	$ 69,119	7.31%	$ 48,507	4.65%	$ 27,868	2.23%
Other	$ 31,791	2.84%	$ 28,547	3.02%	$ 28,336	2.71%	$ 27,809	2.22%

Source: US Department of Labor LM-2 Reports

Table 3.4 UAW Major Categories of Revenues, Selected Years, 2007–2018 (in thousands)[4]

Category	2018		2015		2011		2007	
	Amount	% of Total	Amount	% of Total	Amount	% of Total	Amount	% of Total
Net Revenue	$ 242,313		$ 275,559		$ 245,965		$ 315,633	
Member-Based Income	$ 180,698	74.57%	$ 168,335	61.09%	$ 122,377	49.75%	$ 168,793	53.48%
Investments	$ 28,987	11.96%	$ 66,421	24.10%	$ 91,105	37.04%	$ 95,576	30.28%
Loans Payment	$ 356	0.15%	$ 936	0.34%	$ 915	0.37%	$ 1,230	0.39%
Business Income	$ 198	0.08%	$ 252	0.09%	$ 336	0.14%	$ 398	0.13%
Other	$ 32,073	13.24%	$ 39,614	14.38%	$ 31,230	12.70%	$ 49,636	15.73%

Source: US Department of Labor LM-2 Reports

Table 3.5 UAW Major Categories of Disbursements, Selected Years, 2007–2018 (in thousands)[5]

Category	2018 Amount	% of Total	2015 Amount	% of Total	2011 Amount	% of Total	2007 Amount	% of Total
Net Disbursements	$ 243,815		$ 275,511		$ 245,943		$ 317,911	
Operating Budget	$ 135,098	55.41%	$ 118,890	43.15%	$ 141,176	57.40%	$ 169,910	53.45%
Investments	$ 54,745	22.45%	$ 1,798	0.65%	$ 1,477	0.60%	$ 1,222	0.38%
Benefits	$ 30,777	12.62%	$ 127,623	46.32%	$ 69,659	28.32%	$ 91,510	28.78%
Political	$ 10,397	4.26%	$ 6,087	2.21%	$ 7,704	3.13%	$ 6,869	2.16%
Direct Taxes	$ 6,979	2.86%	$ 7,538	2.74%	$ 7,708	3.13%	$ 8,691	2.73%
Per Capita Tax	$ 2,924	1.20%	$ 3,186	1.16%	$ 2,684	1.09%	$ 5,071	1.60%
Contributions	$ 2,221	0.91%	$ 658	0.24%	$ 3,620	1.47%	$ 1,299	0.41%
Loans Made	$ 510	0.21%	$ 5,139	1.87%	$ 6,825	2.78%	$ 10,655	3.35%
Strike Benefits	$ 209	0.09%	$ 4,291	1.56%	$ 5,113	2.08%	$ 22,663	7.13%
Repayment of Loans Obtained	$ -	0.00%	$ 345	0.13%	$ -	0.00%	$ -	0.00%
Withholding Not Disbursed	$ (45)	-0.02%	$ (44)	-0.02%	$ (24)	-0.01%	$ 16	0.01%

Source: US Department of Labor LM-2 Reports

Note: Net Disbursements = Total Disbursements minus Affiliates minus Members selected years reported) consisted of income from interest and the sale of investments. These totals ranged from just over 11 percent (2018) to more than 37 percent (2011), during which year the UAW sold a considerable amount of investments for income. Transfers and transmittals ranked third in terms of major category of receipts, apart from the miscellaneous "other" categorization. The upshot is that between 2007 and 2015 a significant shift occurred in the funding of the UAW. MBI fell to less than 50 percent but climbed to over 70 percent by 2018. Investment income rose to over 37 percent of net revenue in 2011 and then declined to just above 11 percent in 2018. Revenue from "other" sources, a significant share of which are the "chargebacks," comprised from over 12 percent to nearly 16 percent of net receipts.

The breakdown of disbursements appears in Table 3.5. The UAW's operating budget represented the largest share of expenditures for three of the four years reported, ranging from roughly 53 percent to 57 percent of net disbursements. Interestingly, when the unions operating budget declined as a share of spending, which corresponded with the downturn in MBI, the union's relative spending on compensation rose. It appears that the UAW evidently cut back its administrative expenses in order to preserve as many union employees' jobs as possible.

Gross Salaries (and Allowances) of UAW Officers and Employees

Table 3.6 shows clearly the extensive decline in the number of employees and their overall gross salaries plus allowances and reimbursable expenses. Comparing the year 2000 to 2018, the number of employees dropped from over 1300 to 685, a nearly 48 percent decline. The spending on salaries (inclusive of reimbursements) fell by close to 49 percent. In contrast, the total salary budget for officers increased between 2000 and 2010 but fell sharply by 2015. Between 2015 and 2018, however, spending on officers increased dramatically, rising over 70 percent.

Financial Capacity

We measure the financial capacity of the UAW to represent its members in two ways. First, we calculate a financial capacity ratio by dividing the union's operating budget by its MBI for the years between 2006 and 2018. This ratio shows the operating budget as a percentage of MBI. A ratio above 1.0 signifies that the operating budget is greater than the MBI, which means that the UAW must rely on non-member sources of revenue to pay for its basic operation. Second, we compute the UAW's MBI per member. This shows the amount the union has to spend from its per capita tax on members to pay for representation.

Table 3.7 shows the financial capacity ratios, which indicates that the union's operating budget exceeded its MBI from 2007 to 2014. In 2009, in

Table 3.6 UAW Compensation to Employees and Officers, Selected Years, 2000–2018[6]

Category	2000	2007	2010	2015	2018
Total Employees	1,313	1,044	940	733	685
Total Officers	19	18	25	14	21
Total Salaries	$ 103,000,116	$ 99,894,114	$ 81,844,707	$ 74,349,276	$ 75,353,781
Employee Salaries	$ 100,584,235	$ 97,228,341	$ 78,438,449	$ 72,191,810	$ 71,648,681
Officer Salaries	$ 2,415,881	$ 2,665,803	$ 3,406,258	$ 2,157,466	$ 3,705,100
Top Employee Salary	$ 166,448	$ 166,207	$ 144,433	$ 244,396	$ 189,439
Average Employee Salary	$ 76,606	$ 93,131	$ 83,445	$ 98,488	$ 104,597
Top Officer Salary	$ 145,519	$ 163,075	$ 169,916	$ 170,464	$ 260,243
Average Officer Salary	$ 127,152	$ 148,100	$ 136,250	$ 154,105	$ 176,433
Number of Employees > $100K	311	592	402	439	431
Number of Officers > $100K	19	18	24	14	20

Source: US Department of Labor LM-2 Reports

Note: Total includes gross salary, allowances, official business, and other. Does not include benefits.

Table 3.7 UAW Financial Capacity Ratio, 2006–2018 (in thousands)[7]

Year	Operating Budget	Member-Based Income	Capacity
2018	$135,098	$ 180,698	0.748
2017	$129,179	$ 175,761	0.735
2016	$127,045	$ 182,485	0.696
2015	$118,890	$ 168,335	0.706
2014	$129,102	$ 116,785	1.105
2013	$127,458	$ 115,110	1.107
2012	$132,928	$ 114,997	1.156
2011	$141,176	$ 122,377	1.154
2010	$144,170	$ 119,017	1.211
2009	$161,464	$ 127,494	1.266
2008	$170,783	$ 161,343	1.059
2007	$169,910	$ 168,793	1.007
2006	$174,144	$ 191,219	0.911

Source: US Department of Labor LM-2 Reports

Table 3.8 UAW Per-Member Member-Based Income (MBI), 2000–2018[8]

Year	MBI	Members	MBI / Member
2018	$ 180,698,231	395,703	$456.65
2017	$ 175,761,331	430,871	$407.92
2016	$ 182,485,234	415,963	$438.71
2015	$ 168,335,298	408,639	$411.94
2014	$ 116,785,441	403,466	$289.46
2013	$ 115,110,422	391,415	$294.09
2012	$ 114,997,371	382,513	$300.64
2011	$ 122,377,226	380,719	$321.44
2010	$ 119,016,693	376,612	$316.02
2009	$ 127,493,840	355,191	$358.94
2008	$ 161,342,651	431,037	$374.31
2007	$ 168,792,721	464,910	$363.07

(Continued)

Table 3.8 (Cont.)

2006	$ 191,219,048	538,448	$355.13
2005	$ 197,065,607	557,099	$353.74
2004	$ 206,488,935	654,657	$315.42
2003	$ 214,337,456	624,585	$343.17
2002	$ 209,118,153	638,722	$327.40
2001	$ 217,376,942	701,818	$309.73
2000	$ 223,141,404	671,853	$332.13

Source: US Department of Labor LM-2 Reports

fact, the budget was 126 percent of MBI. After the dues hike in 2014, however, the situation re-balanced itself; MBI has exceeded the operating budget in each year since 2014. In 2018, for example, the operating budget amounted to just under 75 percent of the UAW's intake of MBI.

The per-member MBI is revealed in Table 3.8. It shows the financial challenges facing the UAW beginning with the Great Recession. The per-member MBI dropped from nearly $360 in 2009 to a low of $290 in 2014. It has climbed significantly since. Between 2014 and 2015, in fact, the per-member MBI rose by over $120, or over 43 percent. Once again, this reflects the dues hike of 2014, which has considerably strengthened the UAW from a financial standpoint from its evident vulnerability between 2009 and 2014.

Notes

1 US DOL, LM-2 forms, OLMS.
2 Ibid.
3 Ibid.
4 Ibid.
5 Ibid.
6 Ibid.
7 Ibid.
8 Ibid.

Chapter 4

The Law

Various labor laws regulate the internal affairs of unions, including matters relating to the management and reporting of finances, and the conduct of labor-management relations on both the union and management sides.[1] Other civil and criminal laws of broader scope may pertain to specific instances of misconduct in the domain of labor-management relations. In this case of the UAW and its relations with selected employers, both sets of legal considerations apply. We review the principal provisions of relevant labor laws to put the activities of various union and corporate officials into legal context. We also note the other statutes invoked to charge selected parties with criminal and civil breaches.

Two sets of laws provided the basis for prosecuting various union and corporate officials for their misconduct (see Table 4.1). The first involves labor laws which prohibit employers from offering things of value to union officers and makes it illegal for union officials to accept bribes or to embezzle funds. A second set pertains to various criminal laws which make it illegal to engage in acts of racketeering and fraud, among other things.

National Labor Laws

Enacted in 1935, the National Labor Relations Act (NLRA), which covers most workers in the private sector outside of the rail and airline industries, granted employees the right to unionize and bargain collectively. This enactment facilitated the spread of union representation in a broader effort to achieve a more equitable balance of power between employers and employees, including the latter's labor representatives.[2] The economic mobilization occasioned by World War II accelerated labor's growth.

As unions grew in number and strength, they provoked a sharp backlash.[3] Congressional demands increased to impose limitations on what some thought were excesses in the powers granted to unions under the NLRA, as administered and interpreted. The Taft-Hartley Act of 1947 ensued, passing both houses of Congress after the Republicans gained control in the 1946 midterm elections. Known officially as the Labor Management Relations

Table 4.1 Selected Provisions of the LMRDA (and Amended Taft-Hartley Act)

LMRDA/Taft-Hartley Provision	*Statutory Language*
Report of Labor Organizations Section 201	(b) Every labor organization shall file annually with the Secretary a financial report signed by its president and treasurer or corresponding principal officers containing the following information in such detail as may be necessary accurately to disclose its financial condition and operations for its preceding fiscal year.
Criminal Provisions Section 209	(a) Any person who willfully violates this title shall be fined not more than $10,000 or imprisoned for not more than one year, or both.
	(b) Any person who makes a false statement or representation of a material fact, knowing it to be false, or who knowingly fails to disclose a material fact, in any document, report, or other information required under the provisions of this title shall be fined not more than $10,000 or imprisoned for not more than one year, or both.
Fiduciary Responsibilities of Officers of Labor Organizations Section 501	(a) The officers, agents, shop stewards, and other representatives of a labor organization occupy positions of trust in relation to such organization and its members as a group. It is, therefore, the duty of each such person, taking into account the special problems and functions of a labor organization, to hold its money and property solely for the benefit of the organization and its members and to manage, invest, and expend the same in accordance with its constitution and bylaws and any resolutions of the governing bodies adopted thereunder, to refrain from dealing with such organization as an adverse party or in behalf of an adverse party in any matter connected with his duties and from holding or acquiring any pecuniary or personal interest which conflicts with the interests of such organization, and to account to the organization for any profit received by him in whatever capacity in connection with transactions conducted by him or under his direction on behalf of the organization. A general exculpatory provision in the constitution and bylaws of such a labor organization or a general exculpatory resolution of a governing body purporting to relieve any such person of liability for breach of the duties declared by this section shall be void as against public policy.
	(c) Any person who embezzles, steals, or unlawfully and willfully abstracts or converts to his own use, or the use of another, any of the moneys, funds, securities, property, or other assets of a labor organization of which he is an officer, or by which he is employed, directly or indirectly, shall be fined not more than $10,000 or imprisoned for not more than five years, or both.

(Continued)

Table 4.1 (Cont.)

LMRDA/Taft-Hartley Provision	Statutory Language
Amendment to Taft-Hartley Labor Management Relations Act of 1947 Re Employer Aid to Union Representatives and Labor Organizations Section 301	(a) It shall be unlawful for any employer or association of employers or any person who acts as a labor relations expert, adviser, or consultant to an employer or who acts in the interest of an employer to pay, lend, or deliver, or agree to pay, lend, or deliver, any money or other thing of value- 1. to any representative of any of his employees who are employed in an industry affecting commerce; or 2. to any labor organization, or any officer or employee thereof, which represents, seeks to represent, or would admit to membership, any of the employees of such employer who are employed in an industry affecting commerce; or 3. to any employee or group or committee of employees of such employer employed in an industry affecting commerce in excess of their normal compensation for the purpose of causing such employee or group or committee directly or indirectly to influence any other employees in the exercise of the right to organize and bargain collectively through representatives of their own choosing; or 3. to any officer or employee of a labor organization engaged in an industry affecting commerce with intent to influence him in respect to any of his actions, decisions, or duties as a representative of employees or as such officer or employee of such labor organization.

Act, Taft-Hartley banned certain union practices such as the secondary boycott and closed shop, provided for the mediation of disputes in the case of national emergencies (and more generally as well), and expanded the realm of employee rights vis-à-vis their employers. Significantly, Taft-Hartley also made it unlawful for employers to make payments or give things of value to labor organizations, or officers and employees thereof, except under certain specified circumstances. The Act further required unions to make certain financial disclosures to the US Secretary of Labor, including the compensation provided to officers, dues rates, and other assessments on members, and receipts and expenditures.[4] The law required that financial reports be made available to union members.

By the mid-1950s, public concerns about continuing union excesses in power and reported instances of serious corruption and misconduct led to a set of highly publicized congressional hearings conducted by the US Senate's Select Committee on Improper Activities in the Labor or Management Field.[5] Senator John McClellan of Arkansas, a Democrat, chaired the committee, on which then Senator John F. Kennedy served. Robert F. Kennedy, the namesake Senator's brother, held the position of chief counsel to the committee. The hearings focused on the alleged wrongdoing among several unions, notably the International Brotherhood of Teamsters, the Operating Engineers, Carpenters, United Textile Workers, and Bakery and Confectionery Workers.[6]

After these extensive hearings and subsequent legislative deliberations, Congress passed the Labor Management Reporting and Disclosure Act (LMRDA) of 1959, known popularly at Landrum-Griffin, after the congressional sponsors. The LMRDA amended Taft-Hartley to strengthen prohibitions on financial ties between employers and union, imposed fiduciary responsibilities on union officers, and required the extensive reporting on financial affairs to the US Department of Labor (DOL), which is required to make such reports public. The 1959 statute also provided for a bill of rights for union members, which granted freedom of speech and assembly, equal rights to participate in internal union affairs, and the right to have a say on dues, initiation fees, and other assessments (US Department of Labor, Office of Labor-Management Standards). Of particular interest here are the fiduciary obligations and reporting requirements, to which we turn.

More specifically, Section 501 of the LMRDA defines the fiduciary responsibility of labor organizations, including their "officers, agents, shop stewards, and other representatives." According to Section 501(a), each of these persons is expected "to hold its [the union's] money and property solely for the benefit of organization and its members." In addition, Section 501(c) makes it a crime for any such person:

> who embezzles, steals, or unlawfully and willfully abstracts or converts to his own use or the use of another, any of the moneys, funds, securities, property, or other assets of a labor organization of which he is an officer, or by which he is employed, directly or indirectly.

Such misconduct is punishable by a fine of "not more than $10,000 or imprisonment for not more than five years, or both."

Federal labor law also prohibits employers from providing money or other things of value to labor union representatives. Section 302(a) of the amended Taft-Hartley Act makes it:

> unlawful for any employer or association of employers or any person ... who acts in the interest of an employer to pay, lend, or deliver, or agree to pay, lend, or deliver, any money or other thing of value to any labor organization, of any officer or employee thereof, which represents, seeks to represent, or would admit to membership, any of the employees of such employer who are employed in an industry affecting commerce.

In terms of reporting requirements, the LMRDA stipulates that each labor organization covered by the statute will file a report with the US Secretary of Labor, signed by its president and secretary-treasurer, disclosing information about its officers, location, dues, and finances. Financial reports, required annually, disclose assets and liabilities, receipts, disbursements, officers' and employees' salaries and allowances, as well as loans owed and made during the relevant reporting fiscal year. Section 205(a) requires the US Secretary of Labor to make these reports publicly available and "make reasonable provision for the inspection and examination, on the request of any person, of the information and data contained in any report" filed accordingly. To this end, the US DOL has promulgated various financial disclosure forms (referred to as LM-2, LM-3, and LM-4, which vary in detail depending on the annual level of revenue generated by the covered labor organization). These data are managed by the DOL's Office of Labor-Management Standards (OLMS), which, as noted, makes the reports available digitally through its online disclosure portal. The LM-2 reports apply to labor organizations with annual receipts equal to or above $250,000.

The current version of the LM-2 form requires that labor organizations report the following:

- annual union membership total;
- dues rates;
- beginning-of-year and end-of-year assets and liabilities by major categories;
- receipts from various sources such as dues or per capita taxes, fees, sales of assets and supplies, dividends, and rents, as well as from affiliates and members for transfer or transmittal to affiliated units of the union and to members;
- disbursements by major category of expenditure; and
- salaries and allowances of officers and employees; loans made and receivable; and expenditures made on representational and political functional activities.

The US Secretary of Labor is granted the power to administer and enforce the law. DOL may also investigate any alleged violation of the statute. Operationally, the OLMS and the Office of Inspector General (Office of Investigations—Labor Racketeering and Fraud) conduct the investigation on behalf of the Secretary of Labor, often in conjunction with a US Attorney's office and the Federal Bureau of Investigation (FBI).

Other Statutes

Selected other criminal and civil statutes have borne on these alleged and established incidents misconduct. Perhaps the most prominent in this regard is the Racketeer Influenced and Corrupt Organizations Act (RICO). This 1970 statute provides for criminal penalties for certain activities undertaken within organizations that effectively turn the entities into corrupted enterprises, which take on a life separate from the legal entity itself. It provides for civil enforcement to recoup damages inflicted by participants in the "enterprise."[7] Section 1961 of the statute defines racketeering to include a variety of crimes such as bribery and extortion which are punishable under State laws (if the penalty entails imprisonment for more than one year) or which violate selected other federal laws.

This same section of the RICO statute also defines a "pattern of racketeering activity" as requiring two or more incidents of criminal acts within a ten-year period.[8] It also defines an "enterprise" as any group, association, union, or corporation that is in existence in fact but not as a distinct legal entity. Individuals who combine or conspire to commit racketeering acts in an organizational context may become distinctive criminal "enterprises," effectively taking control of all or part of the legal entity itself. Thus, a union, by virtue of these criminal activities, may become a partially or wholly controlled criminal enterprise, perhaps involving the participation of individuals associated with outside organizations.

Section 1962 of the statute specifies various prohibited activities. It is "unlawful for any person who has received any income derived, directly or indirectly, from a pattern of racketeering activity or through collection of an unlawful debt…" (18 USC 1962(a)). It is further illegal:

> for any person through a pattern of racketeering activity or through collection of unlawful debt to acquire, maintain, directly or indirectly, any interest in or control of any enterprise which is engaged in, or the activities of which affect, interstate or foreign commerce.

Operationally, the RICO statute involves building a case against individuals who conspire to commit wrongdoing, which are termed "predicate offenses." These offenses include, as noted, extortion and bribery, as well as embezzlement, theft, fraud, and money laundering.

A litany of other statutes may be invoked to prosecute wrongdoing in labor-management contexts, though they are of broader application. These include statutory prohibitions on filing false income tax forms, refusing to file tax forms, mail fraud, wire fraud, and financial institution fraud. The US Attorney's office has charged and successfully prosecuted several corporate and union officials for crimes committed under these labor-specific and more general criminal statutes.[9] In addition, as noted, GM had filed a major civil suit, which was recently dismissed by a federal judge, against FCA and other defendants for engaging in racketeering.[10] After the dismissal, also as previously noted, GM filed an amended complaint on August 3, 2020 broadening the scope of accusations and defendants.[11] While the same federal judge dismissed the amended suit, GM has vowed to appeal the dismissal.

Enforcement

Several federal agencies become involved in the investigation and prosecution of misconduct among the parties who perpetrated the wrongdoing in these instances. In the DOL, the OLMS conducts criminal and civil investigations of violations of the LMRDA and other related laws. It investigates embezzlement, false reporting, or threats or use of force or violence to interfere with a union member's exercising legal rights under relevant labor laws. Also, within the DOL's Office of Inspector General, the Office of Investigations (OI)—Labor Racketeering and Fraud is charged with preventing and detecting fraud in the department's programs and operations. The Federal Bureau of Investigation (FBI), lodged with the US Department of Justice, may also participate in the investigation of misconduct involving labor-management relations and internal union matters. The evidence collected by the FBI, OLMS, OI, and OIG may be presented to the US Attorney's office for possible prosecution.

At the OLMS, the agency collected more than 22,000 LM-1 through LM-4 reports in fiscal year 2018, with the LM-1 being a report on labor organization information. The LM-2, LM-3, and LM-4 annual reports required financial disclosures, with the level of detail depending, as noted, on the size of the labor organizations' annual receipts. OLMS completed 223 criminal investigations that year, of which 73 resulted in indictment and 72 in conviction.[12] In a recent annual report, OLMS disclosed that seven individuals had been sentenced to prison for misconduct in the UAW-related scandals.[13]

Notes

1 Jacobs, J.B. (2006). *Mobsters, Unions, and the Feds: The Mafia and the American Labor Movement*. New York: New York University Press; Jacobs & Cooperman, *op. cit.*, Estey et al., *op. cit.*

2 Greenhouse, *op. cit.*

3 Estey et al. *op. cit.*

4 Stein, Emanuel, Union Finance and LMRDA, in Estey et al., *op. cit.*, pp. 130–153.

5 Levitan and Loewenberg, *op. cit.*

6 RICO statute: 18, USC, 371, 1952.

7 Ibid.

8 Jacobs, J.B., & Cooperman, K.T. (2011). *Breaking the Devil's Pact: The Battle to Free the Teamsters from the Mob*. New York: New York University Press: 23–24.

9 Lawrence and LaReau, 2020, *op. cit.*; GM Civil RICO Complaint; *op. cit.*

10 GM Civil RICO Complaint; *op. cit.*; GM Amended Civil Complaint, *op. cit.*

11 General Motors LLC v. FCA US LLC. US District Court, Eastern District of Michigan, Amended Complaint, Case 2: 19-cv-13429-PDG-DRG, August 3, 2020.

12 Office of Labor Management Standards (2019, January). 2018 Annual Report. https://www.dol.gov/agencies/olms/about/annual-reports/2018.

13 Ibid.

Chapter 5

The Joint Training Programs

The Detroit 3's joint training programs with the UAW emerged in the early 1980s in response to the then-crisis besetting the US auto industry.[1] In the 1970s, the US had experienced at least two major energy crises which significantly rose the price of oil and hence gasoline at the pump. In the late 1970s, the country entered a deep recession coupled with high inflation (i.e. stagflation). Between 1978 and 1982, the unemployment rate had risen from 6 percent of 10.5 percent. The annual inflation rate climbed to 11.3 percent in 1979 and peaked at 13.5 percent in 1980.

At the same time, foreign competition in manufacturing mushroomed. Nearly 70 percent of all goods produced in the US faced some degree of international competition. In auto, the companies were woefully unprepared for the onslaught of imports. In 1986, for example, the average number of cars produced per auto worker stood at 11.7 and 16.1 for GM and Ford, respectively.[2] At Toyota, the average number was a comparatively staggering 57.7.

The result of this perfect storm of adversities was a sharp downturn in the already cyclically vulnerable auto manufacturing sector. Between 1978 and 1982, GM's sales fell from over 6.9 million vehicles to just above 4.5 million. At Ford, sales dropped from 3.8 million to under 2.1 million, and Chrysler's decreased by about 560,000 to just about one million during the same period. The companies' combined share of the US market showed a corresponding decrease from 82.5 percent in 1978 to 74.1 percent by 1982. In 1980, the Detroit 3 reported combined losses of $4.2 billion, with a 30 percent fall in sales to the lowest point since 1961. During 1979 and 1980, the companies shuttered 20 facilities which shed 50,000 jobs; parts suppliers laid off another 80,000 with the closure of 100 more plants. The collapse in the US auto industry forced Chrysler to seek federal relief, which came in the form of a $1.5 billion loan in 1979. At the UAW, membership declined from the union's peak of 1,523,888 in 1979 to 1,057,376 in 1983.[3]

The Detroit 3 realized that they had to restructure massively to recover from this sweeping decline. They not only had problems with respect to steep foreign competition, uncompetitive workforce productivity, and economic headwinds but also weaknesses in quality and product performance.

To regain a competitive edge, the companies, each of which was facing a more or less similar set of profound challenges, embarked upon ambitious joint ventures with the UAW. These ventures focused on making improvements in productivity and quality by establishing jointly administered training programs. Each company established such a venture in the early-to-mid 1980s in its agreement with the UAW. In 1982, Ford and GM created their nonprofit corporations, originally established as I.R.S. 501(c)(3) charities. Chrysler established its version of a joint training venture in 1986. These programs evolved into the UAW-Ford National Programs Center (NPC), the UAW-GM Center for Human Resources (CHR), and the UAW-Chrysler National Training Center (NTC).

The collective bargaining contracts between the companies and the UAW specified how these programs would be funded and administered. The 1982 contract between the UAW and GM provided an illustrative description of these funding arrangements:

> It is agreed the Corporation make available to the Executive Board Joint Activities (Executive Board) funding at a rate of 5 cents (50) per hour worked. The funds are to be used to accomplish the objectives noted in the Joint UAW-GM Statement on Job Security and Competitive Edge in the Marketplace (Joint Statement). The Executive Board may commit Board and authorize expenditures to meet the objectives set forth in the Joint Statement with the understanding that no expenditures for capital items will be authorized without approval of the appropriate divisional comptroller or chief financial officer. It is also agreed that payment of fees in services and expenses provided by Union and Corporation representatives to the Board will be authorized, at rates to be agreed upon, by the Executive Board. In addition to the 5 cents (50) per hour worked funding, a sum will be provided by the Corporation to the Executive Board which will average, over the term of the new National Agreement, $6.7 million per month (annual rate of $80 million). These additional funds will be utilized primarily in the plants for current to and expanded training for bargaining unit employees. It is understood that the cost of joint programs, wages of trainees, travel expenses and other training expenses may be chargeable against these additional funds provided the project is approved, in 272 advance, by the Executive Board and the expenses were within the limits so established.[4]

Over the course of their existence, these training entities, which were reclassified as 501(c)(5) nonprofits in circa 2004–2005, had amassed and spent huge sums of money.[5] For example, between 1982 and 2000, the UAW-GM CHR spent $3 billion (to give an idea of size in relation to the UAW, this is an average of approximately $167 million per year, or about two-thirds of the UAW's entire disbursements for 2018, not factoring in inflation). Ford and Chrysler expended $1.3 billion between 1996 and 1999. Each company designed, in collaboration with the UAW, its own administrative structure.

These joint programs, because they were 50% company and 50% UAW, were largely exempt from US Department of Labor LM-2, UAW, and company financial reporting requirements and UAW and company financial controls. As such, UAW members who wanted to find out more about them were often frustrated with the lack of transparency and accountability. Because these joint training centers were funded from negotiated formulae, there was little, if any, market discipline to assure efficiency. Companies apparently didn't have much reason to care so much about what spending was done because the funding was already negotiated and out of the company's control. The UAW may have seen these as joint programs as opportunities to appoint loyal caucus members to joint positions, where working conditions were often better than the factory floor. They also provided the money for the companies to pay the salaries for many UAW International Representatives assigned to that department within the UAW. These joint programs grew and served as a way to grow the UAW. Dissident UAW members were concerned that these joint training centers were influencing the UAW in contract negotiations to the detriment of members.

The training programs across the three companies had joint boards with equal representation of management and union representatives. Typically, the companies' top labor relations officers and the UAW's International Vice Presidents for the corresponding companies became co-leaders of the programs' executive boards. Again, the companies provided funding for the programs based on negotiated formulae. Decisions about operations and expenditures were ostensibly jointly made by these joint boards, somewhat independent of the companies and not formally controlled by the UAW either.

The training programs regularly made so-called "Joint Fund Reimbursements" (JFRs) to the UAW to cover the salaries and benefits of UAW employees assigned to the programs. These JFRs have become referenced as "chargebacks." The training programs have had to make financial disclosures to the IRS using the IRS 990 forms, but they do not have to report LM-2's to the US DOL under the LMRDA. However, the UAW's LM-2 reports do disclose the "chargebacks" made by the training centers to the UAW International. The training programs' 990s do not refer to payments made to the UAW as "chargebacks" but rather classify such expenditures as made for different purposes, depending on the specific accounting practices of programs. UAW members who were critical of the joint training centers were frustrated with the lack of access to detailed and accurate financial and other data regarding their operation.

Selected Data on the Joint Programs

Table 5.1 reports selected data on the NTC for the years between 2014 and 2017. The data are from the NTC's IRS 990 annual disclosures available online. The net assets of the NTC fluctuate, ranging from just about $21 million in 2014 to nearly $22.8 million in 2017. Total revenues, which derive from contributions and grants or from program services, show a pattern of decline, falling from just about $34 million in 2014 to about $25 million in 2017. Total expenses reveal a comparable downturn. The number of employees is reported as 52 in 2017 compared to 68 in 2015. The amount paid on compensation (salaries and benefits plus allowable expenses) ranges from a high of $5.1 million in 2014 to $3.37 million in 2017.

The amount spent on grants (or contributions to individuals and organizations) and conferences shows a dramatic drop, probably due to the publicity surrounding the scandals. Conference spending, for example, fell from over $1.4 million in 2014 to less than $20,000 in 2017. Spending on grants dropped $1.36 million to slightly above $61,000. Legal expenses ballooned from $138,903 in 2014 to $1,129,939 and $1,112,566 in 2016 and 2017, respectively.

The reports list the payments made to the UAW for reimbursements of services provided, which ranged from over $7.4 million to just above $4 million between 2014 and 2017. [As discussed below, these payments are reported as reimbursement for independent contractors of the UAW or sharing paid employees of the union; NPC reports transfers to the UAW for sharing the costs of paid employees; CHR and NTC report payments for UAW independent contractors; NTC reports both expenditures on contractors and transfers.]

Table 5.1 UAW-Chrysler National Training Center (NTC), Selected Data, 2014–2017[6]

Item	2014	2015	2016	2017
Total Assets	$ 29,827,412	$ 33,978,540	$ 29,328,503	$ 31,256,135
Total Liabilities	$ 9,275,374	$ 14,086,957	$ 9,055,325	$ 8,461,414
Net Assets	$ 20,552,038	$ 19,891,583	$ 20,273,178	$ 22,794,721
Total Revenues	$ 33,984,958	$ 30,662,795	$ 28,514,889	$ 25,009,159
Total Expenses	$ 34,220,598	$ 31,310,123	$ 28,172,437	$ 22,487,495
Employees	66	68	63	52
Compensation	$ 5,111,762	$ 3,850,434	$ 3,636,809	$ 3,367,214
Grants	$ 1,360,740	$ 1,607,811	$ 140,750	$ 61,250
Conferences	$ 1,422,159	$ 56,193	$ 12,848	$ 19,902
UAW Transfers	$ 7,444,404	$ 7,169,681	$ 6,287,153	$ 4,051,727
Legal Expenses	$ 138,903	$ 695,400	$ 1,129,939	$ 1,112,566

Source: US Internal Revenue Service Form 990

Three years of IRS 990 filings are available for the NPC (see Table 5.2). Net assets are between $29 million and $34.7 million, with total revenues at $56.2 million in 2016 and $46.7 million two years later. The number of employees is listed at 47 in 2016 but 83 the following two years. Yet, the compensation expenditure is roughly the same across 2016 and 2017, close to $21 million each, with 2018 reporting $17.9 million.

Compared to NTC, the NPC spent a large amount on grants, which totaled nearly $14.5 million in 2016. It lists no expenditures on conferences and zero legal expenses. Payments to the UAW range from $11.6 million in 2016 to over $9.4 million in 2018.

In 2016–2017, the CHR shows net assets between roughly $65.6 million and $71.6 million (Table 5.3). Revenue ranges from over $51 million to under $59 million. The number of employees is just above 100 in each year, with compensation falling somewhere from $35.48 million to $36.03 million. Expenditures to the UAW exceeded $10 million in each year.

Governing Boards and Employee Compensation

We provide more information on the joint training programs governing boards. In the case of the CHR and NTC, a few of the individuals on the boards evidently used their positions for illegal personal gains. The GM CHR lists nine board members in its 2016 report, one of whom served for only part of that calendar year. The co-presidents of the board are the then-International Vice President of the UAW heading the GM department and the highest-ranking corporate officer then on the governing body. Ford NPC lists 12 members on its program's governing board. The highest-ranking

Table 5.2 UAW-Ford National Program Center (NPC), Selected Data, 2016–2018[7]

Item	2016	2017	2018
Total Assets	$ 40,065,718	$ 42,747,813	$ 44,276,052
Total Liabilities	$ 10,969,914	$ 10,796,471	$ 9,514,086
Net Assets	$ 29,095,804	$ 31,951,342	$ 34,761,966
Total Revenues	$ 56,168,599	$ 51,120,082	$ 46,743,489
Total Expenses	$ 54,099,299	$ 48,264,544	$ 43,848,265
Employees	47	83	83
Compensation	$ 21,074,594	$ 20,739,272	$ 17,970,355
Grants	$ 14,472,111	$ 11,949,688	$ 9,436,074
Conferences	$ -	$ -	$ -
UAW Transfers	$ 11,593,000	$ 10,554,000	$ 9,396,000
Legal Expenses	$ -	$ -	$ -

Source: US Internal Revenue Service Form 990

Table 5.3 UAW-GM Center for Human Resources (CHR), Selected Data, 2016–2018[8]

Item	2016	2017	2018
Total Assets	$ 85,774,230	$ 78,841,262	$ 67,989,644
Total Liabilities	$ 14,186,403	$ 13,262,899	$ 8,324,348
Net Assets	$ 71,587,827	$ 65,578,363	$ 59,574,296
Total Revenues	$ 58,732,384	$ 51,032,538	$ 40,378,934
Total Expenses	$ 65,613,937	$ 58,251,321	$ 47,150,270
Employees	102	103	91
Compensation	$ 36,023,485	$ 35,483,824	$ 26,392,678
Grants	$ 1,408,860	$ 900,250	$ (850)
Conferences	$ 64,934	$ 48,310	$ 33,341
UAW Transfers	$ 10,303,437	$ 8,949,517	$ 7,500,669
Legal Expenses	$ 105,995	$ 759,597	$ 4,092,864

Source: US Internal Revenue Service Form 990

corporate and union officials are co-presidents, with four associate treasurers also serving. The NPC's 990s provide no other information about the board members.

At NTC, ten board members are listed, with four of them having term expirations in the year 2015. The co-chairs include the two highest-ranking officers of respective sides. Two co-directors are also listed, both of whom were compensated in the year. Seven of the ten received some compensation during the year.

In 2016, the CHR reported spending about $10.3 million to the UAW for independent contractors. NTC reports spending almost $7.1 million for the same purpose, but also nearly $6.3 million for program support for the union. NPC itemizes just about $11.6 million in payment to the UAW for sharing the costs of paid employees and other expenses with the union.

Grants/Contributions

As noted earlier, the joint programs report the grants/contributions or gifts made to various entities and individuals for various purposes beyond training *per se*. We provide more specific information about these contributions for the programs in 2016 for illustrative and comparative purposes. In that year, NPC reported making over $14 million in grants, while CHR gave roughly $1.4 million compared to about $140,000 for NTC. NPC made seven cash gifts of over $100,000, with the largest being over one million dollars to the Motown Historical Museum. It also made over 40 contributions between $10,000 to $49,999. In contrast, CHR made only 19 contributions between $10,000 and $49,999. Its largest donation was a $500,000

Table 5.4 Joint Training Center Itemized Chargebacks to the UAW: 2013–2018 Calendar Years[9]

Program	2018	2017	2016	2015	2014	2013
NPC	$ 9,885,098	$ 10,391,286	$ 12,692,764	$ 7,425,000	$ 7,411,994	$ 7,503,811
CHR	$ 7,676,000	$ 9,078,294	$ 10,303,437	$ 11,122,713	$ 9,467,525	$ 9,083,368
NTC	$ 3,210,480	$ 6,131,440	$ 7,569,147	$ 7,675,072	$ 4,880,256	$ 4,936,671
Total	$ 20,771,578	$ 25,601,020	$ 30,565,348	$ 26,222,785	$21,759,775	$ 21,523,850

Source: US Department of Labor LM-2 Reports

gift to the United Way of Genesee County, Michigan. NTC gave the bulk of its grants ($100,000) to the Kokomo Community Development project in Indianapolis, IN.

Chargebacks

The UAW's LM-2 reports show the so-called "chargeback" payments made by the three joint training programs to the UAW (Table 5.4). We report the chargebacks made for the years between 2013 and 2018. In each year, NPC made a payment between $7.41 and $10.39 million; CHR's payments ranged from $7.67 to $11.12 million. In the case of NTC, yearly payments extended from $3.21 million to nearly $7.67 million.

We compare the data for 2016 to the information provided in the programs' 990 disclosures for the same year. What is noteworthy is that the chargebacks reported in the LM-2s are more than the items reported for NPC and CHR but not as great as the total payments made by NTC, which includes reimbursement for program services and payment to the UAW for independent contractors [this might be explained at least in part because the IRS Form 990's use the accrual accounting method while the LM-2's use cash accounting method]. However, the amount that the CHR reports for independent contractors ($10,303,437) is very close to the chargeback of $10,343,211 (or within the range of three-tenths of one percent). Ostensibly, the chargebacks are to cover for the costs of compensating for shared employees, or UAW employees assigned to work at the training centers. In the case of the NPC, the nearly $12.7 million in chargebacks is about 9.5 percent more than the amount listed as being paid to the UAW to share for the costs of paid employees. For NTC, the chargeback is 7.3 percent greater than the $7,081,462 listed in program support. It should be noted that as the result of the federal investigations and public scandals, it was found that certain transactions with the UAW in years prior were not proper. As such, in 2019 the UAW settled with NTC and repaid $4,859,216 to the NTC.

Notes

1   Adams, 2010, 2019, *op. cit.*; Brooks, 2020, *op. cit.*
2   Ibid.
3   Ibid.
4   Adams, 2010, *op. cit*, pp. 271–271.
5   Adams, 2019, *op. cit.*; Hyde, P, (2004). *Position Paper Outline: UAW Joint Funds Are Not a "Labor-management Committee" Under 29 USC 186(c)(9) But Are, Rather, Labor Trusts Mandated to Make Audits Available for Inspection Pursuant to 29u.S. C. § 186(c)(5)(B)*, Policy and Law Adviser, Office of Labor-Management Standards, US Department of Labor, Presented to the Office of the Solicitor General.
6   NTC, US Internal Revenue Service Form 990 Disclosure forms.
7   NPC, US Internal Revenue Service Form 990 Disclosure forms.
8   CHR, US Internal Revenue Service Form 990 Disclosure forms.
9   US Department of Labor LM-2 Reports.

Chapter 6

Autos in Bankruptcy

In December 2007, the United States officially entered into an economic recession which ended up being the deepest in the post-World War II period. Technically, it ended in June 2009, but its adverse effects have still ramified.[1] Financial and energy crises preceded the Great Recession, contributing to and magnifying its impact. The economic problems combined to have a particularly harsh effect on auto manufacturing, whose import reverberates throughout the economy. In fact, the auto industry had already entered a slump before the Great Recession, triggered in part by the spike in energy prices which shifted consumer demand from the more profitable truck and Sports Utility Vehicle (SUV) segment of motor vehicles to cars. A crisis eventually fell upon the US auto industry, threatening the very existence of the Detroit 3 (Chrysler, Ford, and GM). To prevent its collapse, as noted, the federal government provided over $80 billion of assistance to GM and Chrysler, both of which declared Chapter 11 bankruptcy in the first half of 2009. Ford had averted a similar fate by having leveraged its entire portfolio of assets, including the symbolically important blue oval logo, to get a massive loan before the financial crisis dried up its line of credit. Each of the companies had to make changes in contracts with the UAW during this period, and Chrysler entered into a consequential alliance with Fiat in order to survive. This alliance evolved into a full-fledged merger several years later, with FCA having recently consummated plans to merge with PSA to become Stellantis in 2021.

The seeds of corruption do not lie in economic adversity, either structural or cyclical, but rather in human frailty. The tumult and turmoil of this exacting period made the auto companies and the UAW more mutually dependent. A labor-management relations confrontation at this critical juncture may have pushed the companies over the edge. The companies experienced massive financial losses, which necessitated widespread plant closures and downsizing. Losing members by the tens of thousands, the UAW faced its own financial problems, which compelled it to shed jobs and restructure its finances.

The Great Recession

A financial crisis triggered by widespread defaults on risky subprime mortgage repayments catapulted the United States in a steep economic downturn. During the 19-month recession, the nation's Gross Domestic Product (GDP) shrank by 4.3 percent; unemployment jumped to 9.5 percent before peaking at 10 percent in October 2009; home prices had fallen 30 percent from peaks in mid-2006 by mid-2009; and the S&P Index dropped by 57 percent between October 2007 and March 2009.

The Crisis in Autos

This economic downturn crushed the US auto industry, whose sales, as previously mentioned, had already dipped. GM and Chrysler had last made profits in 2006, and the three auto companies, in the face of intense foreign competition, had negotiated new contracts with the UAW in 2007 to address their competitive disadvantages in the area of labor costs. The Detroit 3's share of motor vehicle sales in the US had shrunk from 70 percent in 1998 to 53 percent in 2008.[2] In 2008, US auto sales fell 18 percent to 13.2 million from over 16 million in 2007. GM reported losing $30.29 billion in that year. Ford and Chrysler lost $14.6 billion and $16.8 billion, respectively (see Table 6.1).

During 2008, political pressures grew to provide some governmental relief to the struggling auto companies, though there was stiff resistance to such aid.[4] Lawmakers in Washington from states which had significant Detroit 3 auto employment advocated government intervention to prevent more widespread job losses. Indeed, employment in the auto industry had been shrinking for years in the face of rising competition, uncompetitive cost structures, and shifting consumer preferences. The number of hourly jobs in the Detroit 3 combined fell from 408,701 to just 171,742 between 2001 and 2010.[5] Auto executives, in fact, had testified before Congress in December of 2008, pressing the case for financial assistance. GM in particular requested a $4 billion loan to tide it just through the end of 2008 and additional $18 billion in potential aide in 2009. Shortly before leaving office in fact, President George W. Bush revealed a plan to loan $17.4 billion in TARP (Troubled Assets Relief Program) to GM and Chrysler to prevent bankruptcy. Congress had enacted and Bush signed TARP

Table 6.1 Auto Manufacturer's Market Share[3]

Year	Detroit 3	International
1986	72.4%	27.6%
1993	73.7%	26.3%
2007	49.6%	50.4%
2011	46.7%	53.3%

into law a few months earlier to provide up to $700 billion in federal assistance to ailing companies, particularly in the financial sector, where a banking crisis had been in full swing. As shown in Table 6.2, the number of hourly jobs in the Detroit 3 combined fell from 408,701 to just 171,742 between 2001 and 2010.

In February 2009, President Obama established the Presidential Task Force on the Auto Industry, chaired by Secretary of Treasury Timothy Geithner and Larry Summers, then Director of the National Economic Council. The Task Force worked intensely in the early months of the Obama administration to find a path to avoid having to deploy the "B" option, or bankruptcy, for GM and Chrysler. Despite herculean efforts, neither GM nor Chrysler could avoid that fate. In spring 2009, Chrysler and GM entered Chapter 11 bankruptcy. From the perspective of many, including allies of the UAW and lawmakers dependent on auto jobs in their states or congressional districts, it became virtually un-American to contemplate the liquidation of either of these iconic companies, especially one of GM's enormous magnitude.

The major political concern during the efforts to rescue the struggling auto companies centered on preserving jobs in the United States. The auto industry had long been on a downward path in this regard, given the realities of lost market share, outsourcing, offshoring, and job-shedding advances in technology which made the manufacture of motor vehicles with far fewer employees possible. But auto manufacturing has remained a force multiplier in the US economy. Each auto worker generates about 7.6 additional jobs among suppliers, dealerships, and businesses benefiting from their consumer purchasing power.

Federal Assistance

The presidential task force worked with the companies to provide financial assistance and restructure the companies so that they could emerge successfully from bankruptcy. As shown in Table 6.3, the government essentially provided nearly $83 billion in aid to GM and Chrysler, including their financial services units which provided consumers with the wherewithal to purchase a car. GM itself received $36 billion and the GMAC financing unit got $30.6 billion in loans. GM and Chrysler both had to have major restructuring of their debt and

Table 6.2 Detroit 3 Hourly Employment[6]

Year	Employment
2001	408,701
2004	355,961
2007	250,639
2009	169,966
2010	171,742

Table 6.3 Federal Aid to Auto Industry (in billions USD)[7]

Date Announced	Recipient	Amount
12/8/2008	GMAC	5.9
	General Motors	13.4
1/9/2009	Chrysler	4.0
	Chrysler Financial	1.5
4/9/2009	GM	2.0
	Chrysler Holding	0.3
	GM Supplier	2.5
	Chrysler Receivables	1.0
5/9/2009	Chrysler	1.9
	GM	4.0
	GM Warranty	0.4
	GMAC	7.5
	New Chrysler	4.6
6/9/2009	GM	30.0
12/9/2009	GMAC	3.8
	Total	82.8

the liquidating of large swaths of fixed assets (i.e. plants and equipment) and laying off workers (hourly and salaried). Through the bankruptcy process, the Old Chrysler and the Old General Motors emerged as the New Chrysler Group LLC and the New General Motors Company.

More than just labels changed during the brutal restructuring that took place, not only among GM and Chrysler but also Ford, which had to undertake its own rework simply to stay afloat and get out from its heavy indebtedness. GM and Chrysler had to restructure their ownership. In both cases, the US government and the aforementioned UAW Retiree Medical Benefits Trust (RMBT) VEBA became major owners. At GM, ownership broke down as follows: US Treasury (60.80 percent); UAW RMBT VEBA (17.50 percent); Canada/Ontario (11.70 percent); and bondholders (10.00 percent).[8] In Chrysler's case, the ownership required partnership with Fiat, whose CEO Sergio Marchionne was crusading for inter-company consolidation in an industry he regarded as seriously under-performing because of insufficient economics of scales and technological complementarity.[9] The ownership of the Chrysler-Fiat alliance unfolded as: UAW VEBA (67.69 percent); Fiat (20.00 percent); US Treasury (9.85 percent); and Canada (2.46 percent). Parenthetically, Fiat was granted the contingent option of acquiring another 31 percent upon meeting specified criteria.[10]

The companies also exited bankruptcy with significantly different footprints in the US and globally. Under the New GM, worldwide employment had dropped by about 44,500, with 16,000 of these job losses in the US. It reduced its number of plants from 47 to 34, while shedding about 2,300 dealerships. Chrysler trimmed its workforce by 3,000, almost exclusively in the US and dropped one plant while cutting 943 dealerships. While the companies still had large numbers of retirees for which they owed various obligations, notwithstanding the VEBAs, they had reduced their debt burden by 56.5 percent at GM and 41.6 percent at Chrysler. These changes are summarized in Table 6.4.

Labor Negotiations

In 2009, the UAW and the Detroit 3 reopened their contracts to agree to new terms, partially to accommodate developments in bankruptcy but also to continue on the path of lowering labor and production costs. As part of these agreements, the companies and the UAW suspended the cost-of-living allowances (COLAs) and performance bonuses, froze wages for new employees, and pledged not to strike (at least in the case of GM and Chrysler; Ford, which did not undergo bankruptcy, was not able to secure a no-strike pledge; its workers rejected a tentative contract with such a stipulation in 2009 negotiations).[12] In addition, the parties agreed to eliminate the so-called "jobs bank" which essentially guaranteed workers who were laid off from their regular jobs the pay and benefits equivalent to what they were earning while at work.[12]

The UAW consented to another stipulation with the companies as a condition for exiting bankruptcy. That is, the parties agreed to lift the cap on Tier 2 workers set at 25 percent of the hourly workforce in 2007 until the expiration of the contract to be renegotiated in 2015. This agreement allowed the company to hire more Tier 2 workers up to that point just as long as the proportion of Tier 2 workers did not exceed 25 percent at the September 2015 date of expiration. As noted, in 2007, the union had agreed

Table 6.4 The Restructured GM and Chrysler[11]

Dimension	Old GM 2008	New GM 2009	Old Chrysler 2008	New Chrysler 2009
Employment	243,500	209,000	51,000	48,000
Plants	47	34	21	20
Dealerships	5,900	3,600	3,298	2,355
Debt (billion USD)	46b	20b	13.7b	8b
Retirees	531,396	539,350	126,000	130,000
US Production	2,285,733	1,185,661	1,121,498	485,588

Table 6.5 Hourly Labor Costs for Auto Manufacturers[15]

Manufacturer	2007	2011	2015	2019
FCA		$52	$47	$50
Ford	$71	$58	$57	$61
GM	$78	$56	$55	$63
Transplants, Average	$49			$50

to a two-tier wage system, along with the VEBA, to bring the companies into a more competitive position with respect to labor costs. In regard, in 2007, GM's average hourly labor costs totaled $78, including wages and benefits.[13] At Ford, the figure was $71. The foreign-owned US auto manufacturers' hourly equivalent stood at $49. The gap between labor costs for GM and FCA has remained a major obstacle to competitiveness, with the Detroit 3 seeking to reduce the gap in each of the subsequent rounds of bargaining in 2009 through 2019.[14] These labor costs are summarized in Table 6.5.

Notes

1 Rattner, *op. cit.*
2 Schwartz, A. (2011). *A Look Back and a Look Forward.* Center for Automotive Research Breakfast Briefing, November 29; Schwartz, 2015, *op. cit.*
3 US Department of Labor LM-2 Reports; Ford Motor Company, 2015, *op. cit*; Canis et al., *op. cit.*
4 Canis et al., *op. cit.*
5 Ibid.
6 Schwartz, 2011; 2015; Ford Motor Company, 2015, *op. cit*; Canis et al., *op. cit.*; McAlinden, Dziczek, & Schwartz, 2011, *op. cit.*; McAlinden, 2015, *op. cit.*; Canis and Yacubucci, *op.cit.*
7 Ibid.
8 Automotive News, 2019, The UAW-Detroit 3 2019 Negotiations, retrieved July 15, 2020, https://www.autonews.com/assets/html/uaw2019/index.html; Ford Motor Company, 2015, *op. cit.*; Canis et al., *op. cit.*
9 Automotive News, *op. cit.*; Ford Motor Company, 2015, *op. cit.*
10 Automotive News, *op. cit.*; Ford Motor Company, 2015, *op. cit.*
11 Rattner, *op. cit.*; Automotive News, *op. cit.*; Ford Motor Company, 2015, *op. cit.*
12 Automotive News, *op. cit.*; Ford Motor Company, 2015, *op. cit.*
13 Automotive News, *op. cit.*; Ford Motor Company, 2015, *op. cit.*
14 Automotive News, *op. cit.*; Ford Motor Company, 2015, *op. cit.*
15 Rattner, *op. cit.*; Automotive News, *op. cit.*; Ford Motor Company, 2015, *op. cit.*

Chapter 7

FCA, UAW, and NTC

The scandal involving officials affiliated with the FCA and UAW represented a systemic effort to use funds for personal enrichment to create a climate of mutually beneficial labor-management relations that entailed the further misuse of corporate funds. In particular, high-ranking officers, including the CEO of FCA, encouraged and authorized the UAW-FCA National Training Center to channel money to UAW officials for personal expenditures on expensive gifts, meals, mortgages, entertainment, jewelry, clothing, and travel. The scandal involved two successive International Vice Presidents of the UAW, the Vice President of Employee Relations of FCA, and numerous other officials on both the labor and corporate sides. More specifically four FCA officials were involved, as were five UAW officials, plus an independent contractor who had a personal relationship with one of the UAW officials. Several of these officials served on the governing board of the NTC, exercising control over its finances and expenditures.

The late CEO of FCA, Sergio Marchionne, urged the "bribery" of UAW officials to "buy" improvements in the company's labor cost structure to make it more attractive as a potential merger partner with GM, which had been a goal of his for numerous years prior to the commission of overt acts of wrongdoing.[1] Funds were channeled through the UAW-Chrysler National Training Center (NTC) to union officials directly or indirectly through charities or more or less sham companies created to reap the financial benefits of the graft, which totaled over four million dollars over the years between 2009 and 2018. The explicitly expressed purpose of this elaborate and extended scheme was to make the UAW "fat, dumb, and happy."[2] Over the course of time, the temptation to dip into the NTC funds proved irresistible to selected corporate officials, who willingly and flagrantly embezzled money and defrauded the US.[3]

Toward the same end, the UAW-FCA National Training Center arranged to make substantial payments to the UAW in the form of "chargebacks," which exceeded $30 million between 2009 and 2018. The chargebacks, which included a seven percent "administrative fee," reimbursed the union for the salaries of various UAW employees assigned to the training center. Some of these "employees" were ghost workers who performed no duties.[4] FCA officials involved in this arrangement viewed the chargebacks as a "political gift" to the UAW for which the company would derive benefits in negotiating cost-favorable collective bargaining agreements and resolving grievances in a cost-efficient manner.[5] Our focus in this chapter, however, is on the misuse of NTC funds for personal gain by corporate and union officials. We address the genesis of the corporate motivations for this pattern of wrongdoing in a subsequent chapter on GM's racketeering lawsuit against the FCA, which allegedly was morphed into a racketeering enterprise operating for illicit purposes.[6]

The principal organizations involved directly in the scandal include the FCA, UAW, and their joint training program, the NTC. The NTC provided the source of funding for the various schemes perpetrated, receiving its revenue from the FCA based on a contractually negotiated formula. Metaphorically, this represented a situation where the fox was guarding the chickens.

The three major recipients of financial gain were the two highest-ranking officials (Iacobelli and Holiefield) and the girl-friend/spouse (Monica Morgan) of the latter. In the case of Holiefield and Morgan, money was frequently laundered through a charity headed by Holiefield (the Leave the Light on Foundation, LTLOF) and three companies run by Morgan or both Holiefield and Morgan: Monica Morgan Photography, Wilson Diversifed [sic] Products, and Morgan Company A (the joint Morgan-Holiefield firm).[7] With respect to Iacobelli, the NTC made payments to cover various purchases he made with his personal credit cards and either directly to him or vendors performing personal services. Iacobelli encouraged Holiefield and other UAW officials to make liberal use of the NTC-provided credit cards for personal purposes in an overt effort to curry favor with the UAW.[8]

Media accounts of the FCA-UAW-NTC surfaced in 2017, as the ongoing federal investigation, spearheaded by the US Attorney's office in Eastern Michigan, uncovered evidence of wrongdoing.[9] This investigation, aided by the US Department of Labor (DOL) and the FBI, has resulted in eight criminal convictions in this particular situation, seven of which have resulted in prison sentences. The only two individuals mentioned as parties to the scandal who have not been convicted have died: Holiefield, who passed away in 2014, and Marchionne in 2018. The parties have been charged with a variety of crimes and convicted of a subset, usually after extensive plea bargaining. To varying degrees, each of the perpetrators have cooperated with the US Attorney's office, and this has resulted in sentences lower than the guidelines stipulated for the crimes involved. The highest-ranking corporate official convicted across all of the UAW-related scandals is Alphons Iacobelli, VP of Labor Relations at FCA, who was sentenced to five-and-one-half years in prison for pleading guilty to conspiracy to violate the Labor Management Relations Act and filing a false tax return. He has been ordered to make vast restitution.[10]

The magnitude of Mr. Iacobelli's wrongdoing, and the reach of the scandal into broader corridors of the FCA and UAW, is revealed in a statement made by Mr. David Gardey of the US Attorney's office during Iacobelli's August 2018 sentencing. In relevant part, Mr. Gardey stated:

> Your honor, this case is about a calculated effort over many years to break this law [the Labor Management Relations Act of 1947] by under-mining the loyalty of high level UAW officials to the rank-and-file mem-bership of the United States Auto Workers. A corporation, Fiat Chrysler Automobiles, through its executives and in the interest of that coopera-tion, sought to buy labor peace and to soften the zealous advocacy of the union officials by paying bribes to those officials and giving money to the UAW union itself. In this conspiracy Mr. Iacobelli acted in the interest of his employer for which he was well compensated. He was a strategic partner in this conspiracy. But Mr. DuMouchel [Iacobelli's defense attorney] is correct that the conspiracy began long before Mr. Iacobelli and that the payments to union officials by this company and its corpo-rate predecessors did not end in June of 2015 and they began before 2009 in Mr. Iacobelli's involvement in the conspiracy. And there is no question that Mr. Iacobelli has accepted acceptance of responsibility for his crim-inal activity and that he's gone to great lengths to repair and assist the government in rooting out those wrongs.[11]

A partial list of the overt acts of criminal wrongdoing appear in Table 7.1. The timeline of criminal activities suggests that after a period of channel illegal payments directly or indirectly to Holiefield and Morgan, Iacobelli decided to partake himself. After all, Iacobelli, with the explicit or implicit assistance of other corporate and labor officials with connections to the NTC, had caused funds to pay for a home mortgage of over $260,000; numerous trips to vacation spots; luxurious hotel accommodations; lavish meals; designer clothing; jewelry; and furniture. The NTC paid for credit card and other lavish purchases. Other corporate and UAW officials con-cealed the illegal payments to those within the NTC (and their sponsoring organizations, the FCA and UAW) and to government officials in receipt of required disclosure forms and tax filings.

Iacobelli's use of the NTC for personal purchases screamed of greed and hubris. He bought outlandishly expensive fountain pens (at $37,500 each) and a 2013 Ferrari worth more than $350,000, for which he had a personalized license plate [which undoubtedly attracted the attention that created suspicions as to his conduct, inviting investigation by the authorities]. Iacobelli used the NTC to pay for travel by private jet and expensive home improvements.

Based on the evidence provided in testimony given by the defense attorney and the US Attorney's representative at the sentencing hearing, plus the civil RICO complaint filed by GM against FCA and others, it appears that Mr.

Table 7.1 Partial List of Overt Acts of Criminal Wrongdoing Committed by Selected Parties[12]

Parties	Overt Acts
Iacobelli, Holie-field, Morgan, and Others	Between July 2009 and May 2011, Iacobelli and others transferred more than $150,000 from the NTC to the LTLOF
	Morgan used funds to pay for personal purchases at night clubs, retailers, and restaurants
	Iacobelli authorized travel to California at more than $2000 for Morgan
	Between May 2011 and October 2013, NTC, authorized by Iacobelli and others, purchased more than $30,000 in airline purchases for Holiefield and Morgan to such locations as Miami, Las Vegas, and Los Angeles
	June 2011 Iacobelli authorized NTC to pay for Holiefield to stay at Beverly Hills Hotel in California for four nights at cost of $3100 per night
	Between January 2011 and July 2012 NTC transferred, with Iacobelli and others authorization, more than $425000 to Wilson's Diversifed Products, expressly for "relationship building" purposes with Holiefield
	In 2012, Iacobelli authorized Holiefield and other UAW officials to use NTC credit cards for personal purchases
	Durden collected Holiefield's and other UAW officials' credit card statements and instructed the NTC accounting staff not to open the statements
	In 2012 and 2013, Holiefield made over $200000 in personal purchases on the credit cards for such purposes as jewelry, furniture, clothing
	June 2014, Iacobelli instructed Durden to issue NTC check for $262,219.71 payable to MMS Mortgage Services, LTD to cover Holiefield's and Morgan's residence mortgage in Harrison Township, MI
	In circa 2014, a senior assistant to the former president of the International UAW requested records on NTC credit cards of Holiefield and other UAW officials. Iacobelli responded that "We are providing nothing. Just what we reviewed for the binder … in about a month … maybe … We're gonna have fun with these evil people."
	In February and March 2015, Morgan obtained more than $130,000 from Westar Mortgage, Inc. as an equity loan on her residence in Harrison Township, MI
	In May 2012 Durden filed false IRS 990 form for NTC hiding transfer of $122,000 to LTLOF; failing to accurately report $421,960 in funds transferred from NTC to two separate companies controlled by Morgan; and failed to report accurately $20,690 paid to Iacobelli
	NTC transferred more than $17,095 between October 2011 and September 2012 to pay off Iacobelli's American Express charges; transferred $35,000 to use as down payment for two Mont Blanc fountain pens (worth $37,500 each); transferred $96,000 to install a swimming pool, outdoor kitchen, and outdoor spa at Iacobelli's residence in Rochester Hills, MI

(Continued)

Table 7.1 (Cont.)

Parties	Overt Acts
	On May 14, 2013 Durden filed false IRS 990 report for NTC failing to report accurately $246,652 transferred to three Morgan companies; $89,200 transferred to LTLOF; and $148,095 in compensation paid to Iacobelli
	Between October 2012 and June 2015, NTC transferred or paid the following to Iacobelli: $40,684 for Mont Blanc pens; $159,425 for credit card expenses; $375,047 for the aforementioned home improvements (pool, spa, kitchen); $350,000 to purchase a 2013 Ferrari 458 Spider automobile; $403,834 to pay for personal credit card expenses; $44,491 to pay off student loan of Iacobelli relative; $73,000 for landscaping; $337,004 for personal credit card expenses; and $67,500 for personal travel by private jet
	NTC in 2014–2016 paid for numerous expenses, exceeding $40,000 in total, incurred by Norwood Jewell to lead a lavish lifestyle, including meals and open houses that cost $7,569.55; $7,694, among other expenses

Iacobelli did not concoct the scheme to corrupt the UAW in an effort to favor FCA and promote the prospects of a GM merger. He did, however, willingly join the conspiracy, and succumbed to the tantalizing temptation of personal enrichment. As Mr. Iacobelli's defense attorney, Mr. David Dumouchel, stated in the sentencing:

> The factual basis for Mr. Iacobelli's plea is prolixed with detail, about a conspiracy which he joined, an ongoing conspiracy, a conspiracy he didn't design, he didn't come up with. He joined it and there's no way around it either. He knowingly joined it. This conspiracy is described by the government in the sentencing memo with the NTC being an instrumentality and part of a conspiracy to conceal illegal payments under the benevolent guise of training workers and to an effect by company-friendly policies among the UAW leadership or some of them.[13]

Notes

1 GM Civil Rico Complaint, *op. cit.* GM Amended Civil Complaint, *op. cit.*; Iacobelli, Indictment, *op. cit.*; Brown, Plea Bargain, *op. cit.*
2 Ibid.
3 Ibid.
4 Ibid.
5 Ibid.
6 Ibid; Iacobelli, Sentencing Hearing, *op. cit.*
7 Ibid.
8 Ibid.
9 Burden and Snell, *op. cit.*; Howes and Snell, *op. cit.*

10 Iacobelli, Plea Bargaining; Indictment; Sentencing Memorandum; Sentencing Hearing, *op. cit.*; Mickens, Plea Bargain, *op. cit.*
11 Ibid.; Howes and Snell, *op. cit.*; https://uawinvestigation.com/
12 Iacobelli, Plea Bargain, *op. cit.*; Jewell, Plea Bargain, *op. cit.*; Morgan, Plea Bargain, *op. cit.*; Johnson, Plea Bargain, *op. cit.*; Mickens, Plea Bargain, *op. cit.*; King, Plea Bargain, *op. cit.*; Durden, Plea Bargain, *op. cit.*; Brown, Plea Bargain, *op. cit.*
13 Iacobelli, Sentencing Hearing, *op. cit.*

Chapter 8

Solidarity House, Region 5, and Palm Springs

In this chapter, we focus on alleged or admitted union misconduct that occurred at the UAW's Region 5, Solidarity House in Detroit, and Palm Springs, California, where the UAW held periodic regional leadership conferences with the "attendance" of several UAW IEB officers. The basic misconduct centered on the use of union funds for personal gain, or embezzlement, and connected activities in the form of money laundering, fraud, and the filing of false disclosure reports.[1]

The misconduct that occurred involved individuals connected with several entities: the UAW Solidarity House headquarters; Region 5, the UAW Midwest and Southwestern CAPs, and several resorts in California and Missouri, which facilitated various illegal transactions perpetrated by the co-conspirators (see Table 8.1). The purpose was to finance a lavish lifestyle in which the officials embezzled from the UAW treasury to purchase expensive meals, living accommodations, entertainment, and recreation (golf and related accoutrements).[2] Fake "Master Accounts" were created at resorts, including the Renaissance Palm Springs Hotel (RPSH), to conceal the purchases.[3] UAW funds were channeled into the account through falsified vouchers. The UAW officials direct billed the accounts for purchases made by various vendors (restaurants, grocery stores, housing rentals).

UAW Region 5 encompassed 17 states in the western and southwestern United States: Missouri, Texas, Oklahoma, Arkansas, Louisiana, Kansas, Colorado, New Mexico, California, Oregon, Nevada, Arizona, Utah, Idaho, Alaska, Washington, and Hawaii. Its members worked in the auto parts, aerospace, and beverage container industries for such companies as GM, Ford, Lear, Raytheon, Lockheed, and Vought. Region 5 was headquartered in Hazelwood, Missouri, near St. Louis. The former UAW International Union president Gary Jones served as director of Region 5 between 2013 and 2018. He was preceded by Jim Wells and succeeded by Vance Pearson. On December 5, 2019, the UAW International Executive Board voted to merge Region 5 into Regions 4 and 8, effective February 20, 2020.[4]

The principal parties involved in this alleged scheme included Gary Jones, Dennis Williams (who has not been charged at the time of this writing), Vance

Table 8.1 UAW Scandal at Solidarity House, Region 5, and Palm Springs[5]

Dimension	Description
Narrative	The crux of this scandal is the systematic embezzlement of union funds to finance a lavish lifestyle that was concealed as part of regular leadership conferences held by Region 5 in Palm Springs, CA. Three successive Region 5 Directors, including Gary Jones, who eventually became UAW president, conspired to channel union funds to selected resorts who paid for meals, entertainment, housing, and recreation by these three officials and Dennis Williams, and Norwood Jewell. They established "Master Accounts" at these resorts from which the parties could direct bill their expenses, which were falsified to hide their real purpose
Players	Dennis Williams, former UAW President; Gary Jones, former UAW President and Region 5 Director; Norwood Jewell (former International Vice President, UAW); Vance Pearson (former Region 5 Director, UAW); Jim Wells (former Region 5 Director, UAW, deceased)
Organizations	UAW Solidarity House; UAW-FCA National Training Center; Renaissance Palm Springs Hotel (RPSH), UAW Southwest CAP, UAW Midwest Cap, Loews Coronado Bay Resort, Lodge of Four Seasons; UAW Region 5
Time Period	2009–2017
Crimes	Embezzlement; mail and wire fraud; filing false reports; money laundering; aiding and abetting; conspiracy
Financial Value	Over $1.5 million

Pearson, and Norwood Jewell.[6] The overall amount of money used for illegal purposes exceeded $1.5 million. Numerous transactions were involved in this massive embezzlement, as reported in the criminal complaints filed against Vance Pearson by the US Attorney's office on September 12, 2019 in the US District Court for the Eastern District of Michigan. [Additional evidence appeared in the complaints filed against Robinson and Jones.] These transactions, under the alleged crimes committed, are described in Table 8.2.

The criminal complaint itemized several checks and money wires the UAW issued on its accounts in a JP Morgan Chase Bank in Dearborn, Michigan, to the Renaissance Palm Springs Hotel (RPSH) in California, to cover expenses made the by UAW officials. These allotments totaled more than $1 million from August 15, 2014 to June 7, 2017.

The sources of these funds, as noted, came directly from the UAW's general treasury. In fact, a review of the union's LM-2 financial disclosures reveals the UAW made over $1.86 million in disbursements between 2013 and 2018 to several resorts. This included nearly $1.3 million to the RPSH and almost $790,000 to the Desert Princess Resorts in Coronado, California.

To give a flavor of the various specific activities that these funds were used to pay for, the US Attorney's office alleges that more than $83,000 was spent on

Table 8.2 Description of Transactions Report in the Criminal Complaint Filed Against Vance Pearson, Former Region 5 Director[7]

Key Transactions	Embezzlement. [Background: The UAW's Financial Officers Manual states that the union operates a "voucher system" which means that all "order[s] on the treasury" must be attested to by two officers who can verify or "vouch" for these actions. A June 4, 1954 Administrative Letter issued by Walter Reuther which indicates that the UAW had adopted the "AFL-CIO's Code of Minimum Accounting and Financial Controls for Affiliates" which states that "All expenditures should be approved by proper authority under constitutional provision and be recorded and supported by vouchers; providing an adequate description of the nature and purpose of the expenditure sufficient for a reasonable audit by internal and independent auditors."] Embezzled money for personal use through multiple bank accounts in JP Morgan Chase Bank in Dearborn, MI, in which between 2014 through 2017 the union by check or wire outlaid over $1 million to the Renaissance Palm Springs Hotel (RPSH) in Palm Springs, CA; seven checks totaling $1.025 million in amounts varying from $25k to $245k; the LM-2 reports indicated that these payments were made for the purpose of deposits and expenses associated with the UAW's 2014–2018 Region 5 Leadership Conference. This Region 5 Conference typically occurred in January in Palm Springs. The "call letter" indicates that is typically lasts 3–5 days. Pearson and others would submit expenses at vendors to RPSH to pay the debts, which were incurred for housing at villas with private pools and condos in gated communities for select UAW officials. The conspirators used the "master account" as a way to conceal the embezzling of union funds for their own personal use. Upon an in depth review, agents notes language in the contracts regarding the creation of a master account which provided "UAW authorized staff may sign for payments (charge) at local restaurants, golf courses, and additional retail outlets and RPSH will post these charges on the master account". Cooperating Witness 1, and RPSH employee, indicated that the UAW had a "direct bill" or "master account" arrangement which allowed senior UAW officials to deposit UAW funds up-front and run a table for retail, grocery, meals, liquor, cigar and other entertainment expenses at vendors in and around Palm Springs. Expenses were concealed on the RPSH master invoice as "off-site rooms" and "off-site functions." Many of these expenses are not consistent with legitimate union business, were not reported to Solidarity House or on LM reports. Pearson and Union Official C were the individuals who make the underlying billing arrangements. Over $600k was paid by UAW to RPSH To satisfy debts incurred in such businesses as Holly Homes, Desert Princess Rentals, LG Prime Steakhouse, Johnny Cost's Ristorante, Las Casuelas, Indian Canyons Golf Resort, Gary's Sales, and The Tinder Box between 2014 and 2017.

(Continued)

Table 8.2 (Cont.)

UAW paid over $400k to Palm Springs businesses Holly Homes, Desert Princess Rentals, and Home Cleaning Services of America for off-site condos and villas in gated communities between 2015 and 2017 for Pearson and UAW Officials A, B, C, D. Extended stays at villas: 31 days, 63 days; between 2016 and 2018 $60k UAW funds on restaurants for meals outside date of conference; $80k through master billing arrangement for Indian Canyons Golf Resort; $60k for cigar tobacco, humidors, cigar cutters, at Tinder Box in Palm Springs 2014–2018; While invoicing the 2015 conference, CW-2, and RPSH employee, was approached by UAW Official C to conceal expenses by falsely inflating hotel room rentals on the RPSH invoice. However CW-2 refused to cooperate, and was then approached by UAW Official A, who asked CW-2 to lump the expenses together in line items like "outside activities" and "outside housing." CW-2 and RPSH agreed to the compromise, but CW-2 felt personally conflicted, as purpose was to conceal the true nature of the expenditures from its members. UAW HQ paid over $200k and SOUTHWEST CAP over $195k to the Loews Coronada Bay Resort in Coronado, CA for the UAW Region 5 Community Action Program (CAP) Conference. CAP funds drawn from a checking account in Enterprise Bank and Trust in Clayton, MO. Agents found that the Coronado Resort directed over $25k in UAW funds to Access Destinations for high-end meals and excursions. Agents uncovered a similar patter at Lake of the Ozarks, MO; UAW HQ paid over $300k and MIDWEST CAP over $190k to Lodge of Four Seasons in Lake Ozark for union events like the Region 5 Retired Workers IAC Training and Region 5 Staff Meetings. Union advanced money to Four Seasons to offset expenses incurred by UAW officials at outside vendors; $45k golf means and liquor; $75k golf green fees, etc. CW-3 a senior UAW official in UAW Chrysler Department pled guilty to conspiracy to violate LMRA (Taft-Hartley) arising from acceptance and receipt of prohibited payments and things of value from FCA officials. Personal purchases over $40k on credit cards issued by NTC encouraged by FCA. Tasked with shipping Jewell's golf clubs to Palm Springs in about 2015. CW-3 learned that Jewell UAW A and B were staying at private villas in Palm Springs under the pretense of attending a Region 5 conference. CW-3 learned from CW-4 (a senior UAW official who reported directly to Jewell at FCA). CW-4 pled guilty to violating Taft-Hartley, making over $40k purchase with NTC credit cards encouraged by FCA management officials. CW-4 told agents that Jewell and UAW Officials A, B, C, and D and others spent months at Palm Springs paid for by UAW or FAC. CW-5 former UAW officer. CW-6 who served in UAW Accounting Department; "culture of alcohol"; CW-4 and 5 provided records of Jewell's two parties costing more than $50k, funded by NTC, under guise that they were dinners for UAW IEB to showcase the NTC. Thousand spent on premium liquor, cigars, torcedor, spent on mojito tables and decorations of Miami Vice for them.

(Continued)

Table 8.2 (Cont.)

	Money Laundering, False Entries in Union Records, ad False LM Reports. Six checks drawn on UAW bank accounts and issued to RPSH between August 2014 and June 2017. Payment after fraudulent authorization by Pearson and others on UAW vouchers. Representing payments a legitimate conference expense. 40 subsequent payments totaling over $650k made by the RPSH (doing business as HHC TRS Portsmouth, LLC) to the outside vendors. These money laundering transactions made at direction of senior UAW officials, including Pearson and drawn on funds make available through the fraudulent "advances." These payments were undisclosed to the UAW and made to satisfy the lavish personal lifestyles of Pearson and UAW Officials A, B, C, and D, and other senior UAW officials. Schedule of payments provided on pages 36–37 of complaint against Pearson. Similar payments originating from finances accounts of the Loews Coronado Resort and Lodge of Four Seasons. CW 5&6 involved in recordkeeping and filing public financial disclosure forms under LMRDA. They had no idea what the vouchers they approved were concealing. CW-5 signed the UAW LM report and did not believe that the report accurately characterized the expenses. Search warrants executed in August 2019 by FBI, IRS, DOL, including Pearson's home. Found Titleist irons purchased at The Club Porto Cima with UAW funds at UAW Official A home. Also found over $30k in cash from residence from UAW Official A home
Source	Criminal complaint filed against Pearson in Eastern District of Michigan United States District Court September 12, 2019 [Case 2:19-mj-30488]; relevant statutes: LMRDA or Landrum-Griffin, which makes it a crime to file false LM reports and prohibits embezzling union funds or assets by an officer or employee of a union

golf outings by UAW officials between December 2014 and January 2015. Over $660,000 was spent on a total of 45 transactions between September 17, 2014 and November 1, 2018. Payments were made from a "Master Account" set up at RPSH to such service providers as Holly Homes, Desert Princess, Indian Canyons, Gary's Sales, Tinder Box, Johnny Costas, and LG Prime. UAW officials ate expensive meals, bought clothing, consumed extravagantly priced liquor, wine, and cigars, and rented private villas for extended stays during the winter months. To cover these impermissible expenses, UAW treasury money was laundered and false reports were filed with the US Department of Labor to mask the real purposes behind these expenditures.

Among a few of the "outrageous" purchases made were:

- Eight Titleist 716 AP1 Irons for $896;
- Over $8,000 for spa treatments;

- Over $1,000 for local gun range;
- Over $3,000 on merchandise at a hotel store;
- $227 Crown Royal Reserve; $175 Crystal Head Vodka; $200 Belvedere Vodka; and
- Over $2,000 for excursions to the San Diego Zoo and horseback riding on the beach.[8]

In practice, this scheme of embezzlement involved corrupting selected resorts, such as RPSH, to file false vouchers to the UAW, disguising requests for spending as "outside [leadership conference] activities" or "outside housing." The UAW would transfer money to the RPSH, which would deposit it to a "Master Account." UAW officials would the charge their various expenses to the Master Account. False information would be feed to UAW staff processing these transactions and filing disclosure reports under the LMRDA. During its investigation of these activities, the US Attorney's office benefited from having at least six cooperating witnesses, including several who worked for the UAW. One cooperating witness (CW-5, according the pertinent criminal complaint), a former UAW officer, stated that:

> the UAW's accounting department cut the checks based on the representation that they [the vouchers] were legitimate expenses made for legitimate union conferences. CW-5 did not believe that the union's LM reports gave an accurate picture of expenses surrounding the UAW Region 5 Leadership Conference and the UAW Region 5 CAP conference based on vouchers submitted by UAW Region 5.[9]

UAW Midwest and Southwestern CAPs

Between 2010 and 2019, another UAW official, Eugene "Nick" Robinson, who served during this period as president of the UAW Midwest CAP, participated with other UAW officials in Region 5 and at the UAW International to divert more than $1.5 million in funds from the UAW, UAW Midwest CAP, and UAW Southwest CAP for personal uses. These funds were embezzled through false pretenses to subsidize "the lavish lifestyles to which these [UAW] officials became accustomed."[10] For example, between January and December 2017, Robinson, Pearson, and other UAW officials transferred $539,608 in funds from the UAW, UAW Midwest CAP, and UAW Southwest CAP to four resorts, including the RPSH, Lodge of Four Seasons, and Loews Coronado Bay Resort. During the same time period, they diverted $292,852 in these UAW-connected funds held in the resorts for their personal benefit, including $129,336 for luxury condominiums and villas; $46,588 for expensive meals; $80,904 for golf green fees; $15,274 for cigars and ancillary items; and $18,750 for spa services, clothing, musicals, and amusement park tickets.

To show the extent of the parties' awareness of their wronging, the criminal complaint against Eugene Robinson describes the following chain of events:

1   In or about late 2017, UAW Official A advised EUGENE N. ROBINSON that they needed to halt the cash embezzlement portion of the conspiracy because of the ongoing federal criminal investigation of the United Auto Workers union and because of a new UAW position being taken by UAW Official A.

2   In or about January 2019, in a meeting among EUGENE N. ROBIN-SON, UAW Official A, and Vance Pearson, UAW Official A promised to provide a sham job to the relative of EUGENE N. ROBINSON in order to "take care of" the relative if ROBINSON agreed to falsely take sole responsibility for the UAW Midwest CAP cash embezzlement portion of the conspiracy, thereby attempting to protect UAW Official A from federal criminal prosecution.

3   During a meeting in or about March 2019, EUGENE N. ROBINSON and UAW Official A discussed the government's investigation and the sham job for ROBINSON's relative. During that meeting, UAW Official A and EUGENE N. ROBINSON also discussed whether the government had obtained documents from the union and the hotels relating to the embezzlement scheme. UAW Official A told Eugene N. Robinson that he (UAW Officials A) wished they "burned the records."[11]

Notes

1   USA v. Gary Jones, Criminal Complaint, Second Superseding Information, February 27, 2020, Criminal No. 19–20726, United States District Court Eastern District, Southern Division; USA v. Vance Pearson, Criminal Complaint, September 12, 2019, Case No. 2: 19-mj-30488, United States District Court Eastern District, Southern Division; USA v. Eugene N. Robinson, Plea Bargain, March 2, 2020, Case No. 19-cr-20726, United States District Court Eastern District Michigan, Southern Division; GM LLC, General Motors Company v. FCA, Alphons Iacobelli, Michael Durden, and Michael Brown, Civil Complaint, November 20, 2019, Case 2: 19-cv-13429, United States District Court Eastern District, Southern Division; GM LLC v. FCA, Dennis Williams, Joseph Ashton, Alphons Iacobelli, Jerome Durden, Michael Brown, First Amended Complaint, Demand for Jury Trial, August 3, 2020, No. 19-cr-13429, United States District Court Eastern District Michigan, Southern Division.

2   Ibid.

3   Ibid.

4   Thibodeau and Howes, 2019, op. cit.

5   USA v. Gary Jones, Criminal Complaint, Second Superseding Information, February 27, 2020, Criminal No. 19–20726, United States District Court Eastern District, Southern Division; USA v. Vance Pearson, Criminal Complaint, September 12, 2019, Case No. 2: 19-mj-30488, United States District Court Eastern District, Southern Division; USA v. Eugene N. Robinson, Plea Bargain, March 2, 2020, Case No. 19-cr-20726, United States District Court Eastern District Michigan, Southern Division; GM LLC, General Motors Company v. FCA, Alphons Iacobelli, Michael

Durden, and Michael Brown, Civil Complaint, November 20, 2019, Case 2: 19-cv-13429, United States District Court Eastern District, Southern Division; GM LLC v. FCA, Dennis Williams, Joseph Ashton, Alphons Iacobelli, Jerome Durden, Michael Brown, First Amended Complaint, Demand for Jury Trial, August 3, 2020, No. 19-cr-13429, United States District Court Eastern District Michigan, Southern Division.

6 Robinson, Criminal Complaint, *op. cit.*; Jones, Criminal Complaint, *op. cit.*; Pearson, Criminal Complaint, *op. cit.*

7 USA v. Gary Jones, Criminal Complaint, Second Superseding Information, February 27, 2020, Criminal No. 19–20726, United States District Court Eastern District, Southern Division; USA v. Vance Pearson, Criminal Complaint, September 12, 2019, Case No. 2: 19-mj-30488, United States District Court Eastern District, Southern Division; USA v. Eugene N. Robinson, Plea Bargain, March 2, 2020, Case No. 19-cr-20726, United States District Court Eastern District Michigan, Southern Division; GM LLC, General Motors Company v. FCA, Alphons Iacobelli, Michael Durden, and Michael Brown, Civil Complaint, November 20, 2019, Case 2: 19-cv-13429, United States District Court Eastern District, Southern Division; GM LLC v. FCA, Dennis Williams, Joseph Ashton, Alphons Iacobelli, Jerome Durden, Michael Brown, First Amended Complaint, Demand for Jury Trial, August 3, 2020, No. 19-cr-13429, United States District Court Eastern District Michigan, Southern Division.

8 Ibid.

9 Ibid.

10 Ibid.

11 Ibid.

Chapter 9

UAW@GM CHR

The scandalous behavior at the UAW-GM Center for Human Resources (CHR) involved three principals, each affiliated with the UAW. Each has pleaded guilty to two crimes: (1) conspiracy to commit honest services fraud and (2) conspiracy to commit money laundering. The criminal activities occurred between 2006 and July 1, 2018.[1] The three principals are: Joseph Ashton, identified as Union Official 1 in certain criminal complaints, who was the former International Vice President of the UAW in charge of the GM Department; Michael Grimes, a former senior UAW official, who served as an Administrative Assistant to the International VP GM Director; and Jeffrey Pietrzyk, who was another senior UAW official. Each of these officials was connected with the GM CHR, with Ashton and Grimes serving on the Executive Board of Joint Activities, which administered the CHR.

These union officials participated in schemes to shake down vendors to give kickbacks for contracts awarded through the UAW-GM CHR. Four major contracts provided the basis for these kickbacks (or bribes, as some of the money funneled by the vendors to the officials was used to protect the prospect of future business). Table 9.1 lists the main transactions involved in a pattern of blatant extortion.

Table 9.1 UAW-GM CHR Scandal Contracts[2]

Date(s)	Contract
2006	Contract issued to Vendor A to produce 23,000 watches; $60,000 kickback given to Grimes
2010–2018	Consulting fee given to Vendor A for total of $900,000 in periodic fees
2011	Contract of $6 million given to Vendor A to produce 50,000 jackets for GM workers; $830,000 in kickbacks given to Grimes
2016	Contract of $5.8 million given to produce 55,000 backpacks for GM workers; Grimes given $500,000 in kickbacks
2012–2015	Contract of $3.973 million given to produce 58,000 watches; $250,000 given to Ashton and $100,000 to Pietrzyk and Grimes

In 2006, Michael Grimes recommended Vendor A to provide the UAW-GM CHR with 23,000 custom-made watches. These watches were to be given to UAW workers at one of GM's powertrain divisions. Vendor A, along with his wife and other partners, owned and operated a set of companies that produced custom-made logo products. Most of the Vendor A's business came from the UAW and the joint CHR; the vendor provided clothing and accessories. According to the US Attorney's office August 9, 2019 complaint against Grimes, "Vendor A also owned and operated 'brick and mortar' clothing/voucher stores controlled by the UAW GM Department inside multiple GM manufacturing plants throughout the United States." Clearly, Vendor A depended on the UAW for financial survival, putting it into a potentially vulnerable position.

At this time, Michael Grimes was evidently buying housing property in Rose Township, Michigan. To finance this purchase, Grimes demanded that Vendor A "loan" him the money. Vendor A initially refused, but Grimes then threatened to cancel the contract. Vendor A, feeling the pressure of financial dependency, assented to the demand and agreed to pay $60,000 for the mortgage. A "consulting agreement" was nominally reached between Grimes and Vendor A to hide the transaction. The agreement provided that a $60,000 lump-sum payment be made to Grimes by Vendor A. In return for this "quid," the "quo" was the promise by Grimes to get the watch contract for Vendor A and to "ensure the retention and maintenance of Vendor A's retail stores in the GM plants and secure future business contracts between Vendor A and the UAW-GM Department." Thus, the kickback also morphed into a bribe for future business. Payment was rendered in November 2006.

This $60,000, however, by no means satisfied Grimes' appetite for graft. Grimes extorted another lucrative consulting arrangement of a longer-term nature. Specifically, Vendor A promised to pay Grimes $1,800 a month as a "consultant" for an indefinite period of time, a figure which eventually rose to $3,800 a month. These payments continued until Grimes retired from the UAW on July 1, 2018. To mask this scheme of monthly bribery, Vendor A made payments to a "sham" company named "KKG Consulting," which was owned by a "relative" of Grimes.

Twenty-seven payments resulted from this consulting arrangement, totally nearly $900,000 payable to Grimes' relative or KKG Consulting during the period from November 2010 to October 2017. Once again, however, the appetite for more was merely whetted.

The opportunity for more criminal largesse arose in 2011, when Union Official 1 (reportedly Joseph Aston, the International VP and head of the GM Department, which included the CHR) made a proposal to buy 50,000 "Team UAW-GM" jackets for all GM plant employees. Grimes recommended Vendor A as a sole source provider. UAW-GM CHR awarded the roughly $6 million contract to Vendor A, after which Union Official 2 (reportedly Jeffrey Peirtrzyk) informed Grimes that Ashton wanted a cut of the proceeds. Unions Official 2 instructed Grimes to demand the Vendor A kick back about

$300,000 for Union Official 1. For six months in 2012, Grimes demanded payment in cash from Vendor A. Grimes delivered the payments from Vendor A to Union Official 2, who forwarded the money to Union Official 1. Of the $300,000 in kickbacks/bribes, Union Official 1 gave $30,000 to Union Official 2. This lucrative scheme proved too tempting for Grimes to resist another opportunity for personal enrichment.

Accordingly, Grimes demanded that Vendor A pay him $525,000 in kickbacks. Grimes wanted the money to purchase a house in Fenton, Michigan. Vendor A, as was the case with the jackets, initially refused. Grimes threated cancellation of the contract, and also increased his financial demands. Vendor A succumbed to the pressure and paid Grimes $530,000 in a cashier's check made payable to Grimes' relative. The money was used to pay off the balance owed on land contract for the house in Fenton.

Bear in mind at this point that Grimes had already received illegal payments from Vendor A to finance two major housing purchases and was also receiving a monthly consulting fee of a minimum of $1,800 (for doing nothing in return promising to direct more business to Vendor A). Having gotten away with these transactions for nearly 10 years by 2016, Grimes recommended Vendor A as a sole source contractor to provide 55,000 backpacks to UAW workers. The contract was for $5.8 million. Emboldened, Grimes initially demanded a $1 million kickback from Vendor A, which must have caused considerable sticker shock. Vendor A did not go along with this total amount, but did agree to a lesser $500,000 kickback. Vendor A made various payments to the fictitious KKG Consulting to hide the purpose of the checks.

A few years before the backpack kickback, each of the three principals had had an opportunity to partake in a second watch-kickback scheme but with a different vendor, labeled Vendor B. Vendor B was a chiropractor located in Philadelphia, PA and southern New Jersey. He had Union Official 1 as a patient. In August 2012, Vendor B started a business to sell US-manufactured custom-made watches. The US Attorney's complaint against Grimes stated that the only income Vendor B's watch business generated was from the UAW and CHR.

Union Official 1 had persuaded Vendor B in 2010 to loan $250,000 to a construction company owned by one of his (Official 1) associates. In March 2012, the construction company defaulted on the loan repayments. Union Official 1 offered Vendor B a way to recoup his losses. The plan was to have Vendor B set up a company to sell watches. Union Official I aided Vendor B in locating a manufacturer of watches in late 2012 and early 2013. He negotiated with manufacturer an agreement in which Vendor B would pur-chase 58,000 customized watches for $2,288,200, or a unit price of $42.90. Union Official 1 then had Vendor B bid for the UAW-GM CHR contract to purchase 58,000 watches to distribute to the entire UAW-GM workforce. The bid was for $3,973,000, or $68.50 per watch and went to Union Official 2. Both union officials used their influence to get the bid approved, which it was by the CHR on April 13, 2013 for the $68.50 unit price. In partial payment of the awarded contract, CHR wired a payment to Vendor B of $1,973,000 on May 1, 2013. Soon afterwards, Union Official 1 demanded a kickback of $250,000 from Vendor B.

Vendor B agreed to this demand and began delivering cash payments on a regular basis to Union Official 1's house in $5,000 to $30,000 installments between May 2013 and early 2015. In 2016, Vendor B made additional payments were deposited into Union Official 1's personal checking account. To share the wealth, Union Official 1 directed that Vendor B make kickbacks to Union Official 2. These payments, which totaled more than $130,000, were made in amounts varying from $10,000 to $25,000 and were disguised on the memo lines of the checks as payments for "antique furniture" or "furniture." These payments continued through the summer of 2016. Union Official 2 accepted payments from Vendor B, some of which were shared with Michael Grimes. The payments from Vendor B stopped at Union Official 1's request because news reports had appeared in the fall of 2016 about the federal investigation into corruption involving the UAW and FCA in connection with their joint training center.

Ashton, Grimes, and Pietrzyk have pleaded guilty. Each pled guilty to Conspiracy Commit Hones Services Wire Fraud and Conspiracy to Commit Money Laundering. Grimes pleaded guilty on September 4, 2019 for conspiring in criminal activities involving at least $1.5 million between 2006 through 2018. Pietrzyk pled guilty on October 22, 2019, for crimes committed between 2011 through 2018 involving at least $250,000. Ashton pled guilty on December 5, 2019, for crimes committed between 2012 through 2016 involving at least $250,000.[3]

Notes

1 USA v. Joseph Ashton, Criminal Complaint, November 6, 2019, Case 5: 19-cr-20738, United States District Court Eastern District, Southern Division; USA v. Michael Grimes, Plea Agreement, September 3, 2019, Case No. 19-cr-20520, United States District Court Eastern District, Southern Division; USA v. Jeffrey Pietrzyk, Criminal Complaint, Case 2: 19-CR-20630, September 20, 2019, United States District Court Eastern District, Michigan, Southern Division; GM Amended Civil Complaint, *op. cit.*

2 USA v. Gary Jones, Criminal Complaint, Second Superseding Information, February 27, 2020, Criminal No. 19–20726, United States District Court Eastern District, Southern Division; USA v. Vance Pearson, Criminal Complaint, September 12, 2019, Case No. 2: 19-mj-30488, United States District Court Eastern District, Southern Division; USA v. Eugene N. Robinson, Plea Bargain, March 2, 2020, Case No. 19-cr-20726, United States District Court Eastern District Michigan, Southern Division; GM LLC, General Motors Company v. FCA, Alphons Iacobelli, Michael Durden, and Michael Brown, Civil Complaint, November 20, 2019, Case 2: 19-cv-13429, United States District Court Eastern District, Southern Division; GM LLC v. FCA, Dennis Williams, Joseph Ashton, Alphons Iacobelli, Jerome Durden, Michael Brown, First Amended Complaint, Demand for Jury Trial, August 3, 2020, No. 19-cr-13429, United States District Court Eastern District Michigan, Southern Division.

3 Ibid.

Chapter 10

GM's RICO Case Against FCA

On November 20, 2019, GM filed suit against FCA and three of its former corporate officials in the United States District Court, Eastern District of Michigan, Southern Division.[1] It charged that the defendants violated the Racketeer Influenced and Corrupt Organizations (RICO) Act by engaging in a pattern of racketeering activities to bribe UAW officials and corrupt the union for the purpose of gaining economic advantage for FCA relative to its competitors which bargained with the UAW. GM filed the complaint seeking relief in the form of recovery of financial damages suffered as a result of the financial advantages FCA derived from corrupting the union.[2] In early July 2020, a federal district court judge dismissed the case, after having ordered the CEOs of FCA and GM to meet to resolve their differences, a mandate which was enjoyed by a US Court of Appeals.[3] On August 3, 2020, GM filed an amended civil RICO complaint, having added Dennis Williams, the former UAW International President, as a defendant and charging several FCA and UAW officials with having been corrupted by secret offshore bank accounts financed by FCA.[4]

This specific scandal centered on corporate and union officials using the joint UAW-FCA National Training Center (UAW-FCA NTC) to channel money to enrich the lives of several individuals who have since been convicted of crimes. Corporate officials apparently bribed union officials to tilt the labor-management relationship between the FCA and the UAW to the company's financial advantage. Through a scheme of bribery and financial subsidization of the UAW through the UAW-FCA NTC, corporate and union officials allegedly participated in racketeering activities in violation of the RICO Act and the Taft-Hartley Act of 1947. They manifest two non-legal entities or enterprises (the FCA-Control Enterprise, which was in effect the UAW, and the UAW-FCA NTC Enterprise) to conduct their unlawful scheming. Corporate officials sought to make the UAW "fat, dumb, and happy" through the illegal diversion of millions of dollars in corporate funds to union officials and the UAW treasury.[5] In the process, some of these corporate officials allegedly enriched themselves while corrupting the institutional integrity of the company.[6]

We review the pertinent federal statutes, the parties and organizations involved in the scandal, the various predicate and overt acts committed in furtherance of the crimes (alleged and convicted), the magnitude of financial improprieties, and the disposition of the criminal and civil charges at this point. Our focus is twofold: (1) the various schemes which fall under the rubric of bribery or embezzlement which redounded to the financial benefit of corporate and union officials; and (2) the use of funds from the UAW-FCA National Training Center to subsidize the operations of the UAW and thus further compromise its institutional integrity. We rely on information obtained from the various criminal complaints, convictions, and news reports on relevant activities, in addition to financial disclosures made by the UAW and the UAW-FCA National Training Center.

Relevant Statutes

The relevant statutes in this particular situation include the Racketeer Influenced and Corrupt Organizations (RICO) Act, which was part of the Organized Crime Act of 1970. It stipulates the penalties for engaging in racketeering activity and identifies the predicate offense of such conduct. In so doing, it defines a racketeering "enterprise." In this particular case, corporate and union officials allegedly participated in racketeering activities through two distinctive enterprises use to commit acts of bribery, embezzlement, fraud (including mail and wire), and the unlawful corruption of a union's officials and institution. The alleged conspiracy resulted in their personal enrichment and tainting the collective bargaining process to the advantage of the corporation with which the UAW negotiated labor-management contracts. The RICO Act also made incorporated violations of the Labor Management Relations Act of 1947 as a basis for charging corporate and union officials with RICO violations. Two criminal enterprises emerged in this pattern of racketeering activities: the FCA-Control Enterprise (in reality the UAW) and the UAW-FCA National Training Center Enterprise.

The RICO Act charges against the conspirators revolved around section 1962(a-d) of title 18 of the United States Code (USC), which, broadly speaking, made it unlawful for a person to participate in or derive financial reward from racketeering activities such as bribery, embezzlement, and fraud (including mail and wire):

(a) It shall be unlawful for any person who has received any income derived, directly or indirectly, from a pattern of racketeering activity or through collection of an unlawful debt in which such person has participated as a principal within the meaning of section 2, title 18, United States Code, to use or invest, directly or indirectly, any part of such income, or the proceeds of such income, in acquisition of any interest in, or the establishment or operation of, any enterprise which is engaged in, or the activities of which affect, interstate or foreign commerce....

(b) It shall be unlawful for any person through a pattern of racketeering activity or through collection of an unlawful debt to acquire or maintain, directly or indirectly, any interest in or control of any enterprise which is engaged in, or the activities of which affect, interstate or foreign commerce.

(c) It shall be unlawful for any person employed by or associated with any enterprise engaged in, or the activities of which affect, interstate or foreign commerce, to conduct or participate, directly or indirectly, in the conduct of such enterprise's affairs through a pattern of racketeering activity or collection of unlawful debt.

(d) It shall be unlawful for any person to conspire to violate any of the provisions of subsection (a), (b), or (c) of this section.

The term "enterprise" is defined as any individual, association, corporation, or union or association of individuals which exist in fact but not as a separate legal entity. Enterprises in effect represent the criminally motivated connections used to commit unlawful activities.

The RICO Act also defines racketeering activity to include violations of section 302 of the Taft-Hartley Act of 1947, which states in relevant part:

(a) Payment or lending, etc., of money by employer or agent to employees, representatives, or labor organizations

It shall be unlawful for any employer or association of employers or any person who acts as a labor relations expert, adviser, or consultant to an employer or who acts in the interest of an employer to pay, lend, or deliver, or agree to pay, lend, or deliver, any money or other thing of value—

(1) to any representative of any of his employees who are employed in an industry affecting commerce; or

(2) to any labor organization, or any officer or employee thereof, which represents, seeks to represent, or would admit to membership, any of the employees of such employer who are employed in an industry affecting commerce; or

(3) to any employee or group or committee of employees of such employer employed in an industry affecting commerce in excess of their normal compensation for the purpose of causing such employee or group or committee directly or indirectly to influence any other employees in the exercise of the right to organize and bargain collectively through representatives of their own choosing...

Another noteworthy legal provision not applied to this case nonetheless merits note for it goes to the heart of the notion that there was an FCA-Controlled Enterprise in the UAW, which received sizable amounts of revenue from the company.[4] Specifically, section 8(a)(1) and 8(a)(2) of the National Labor Relations Act, as amended, prohibits employers from interfering in the formation and administration of labor organizations:

> (a) UNFAIR LABOR PRACTICES BY EMPLOYER. It shall be an unfair labor practice for an employer: (1) to interfere with, restrain, or coerce employees in the exercise of the rights guaranteed in section 157 of this title;(2) to dominate or interfere with the formation or administration of any labor organization or contribute financial or other support to it...

The Parties

The parties involved in this case include the plaintiffs, defendants, and so-called "non-party" individuals and organizations (see Table 10.1). The plaintiffs are corporate entities of General Motors, which claim to have suffered severe financial damages from a pattern of racketeering activities among individuals involved in two "enterprises," which are the illegally contrived devices through which such activities were channeled: the FCA-Control Enterprise (which is the UAW) and the FCA-NTC Enterprise, which is the joint training center. The defendants include corporate entities affiliated with FCA/Chrysler and several officials of FCA/Chrysler: Alphons Iacobelli, former Vice President of Employee Relations of FCA; Jerome Durden, former Financial Analyst in the FCA/Chrysler Corporate Accounting Department; and Michael Brown, the former Director of Employee Relations at FCA/Chrysler.

Several other non-party actors, in addition to the FCA-Control Enterprise and FCA-NTC Enterprise, were involved in the scandal from both the UAW and FCA/Chrysler: Sergio Marchionne (deceased), former CEO of FCA/Chrysler; General Holiefield (deceased), former International Vice President, UAW; Dennis Williams, former International President of UAW; Norwood Jewell, former International Vice President, UAW; Virdell King, former senior official of UAW Chrysler Department; Nancy Johnson, former administrative assistant to Norwood Jewell; and Keith Mickens, former senior official of UAW Chrysler Department. Three other non-party organizations were associated with these alleged criminal schemes, each one of which was connected with either General Holiefield or his girlfriend/spouse, Monica Morgan, at the time: Wilson's Diversifed [sic] Products; Monica Morgan Photography; and Leave the Light on Foundation (LTLOF).

Table 10.1 The Parties and Significant "Others" in Original Civil RICO Complaint[9]

Plaintiffs

General Motors LLC

General Motors Company "GM Company" or "New GM"

Defendants

FCA Group [FCA US LLC; formerly Chrysler Group LLC]

Fiat-Chrysler Automobiles NV [formerly Fiat]

Alphons Iacobelli	Vice President of Employee Relations at FCA and Co-Chairman of the NTC and its Joint Activities Board from 2008–2015; pled guilty on January 22, 2018 to subscribing a false tax return; conspiracy to violate the Labor Management Relations Act; sentenced to 66 months in prison; $10,000 fine; and ordered to pay $835,523 in restitution
Jerome Durden	Financial Analyst at Chrysler and FCA in Corporate Accounting Department since 1985; in 2008 assigned by Chrysler to be Controller of the NTC and Secretary of the NTC Joint Activities Board; pled guilty on August 8, 2018 to failure to file tax returns and conspiracy to defraud the US; sentenced to 15 months in prison and order to pay $8,811 in restitution
Michael Brown	Director of Employee Relations at Chrysler and FCA 2009–2016; Co-Director of NTC; pled guilty on May 25, 2018 to misprision of a felony; sentenced to one year and one day in prison and fined $10,000

Significant Non-Parties and Other Entities

Sergio Marchionne (deceased)	CEO of Fiat and later FCA NV from 2004–2018: Chairman and CEO of FCA (2014–2018); Chair (2011–14) and CEO (2009–14) of Chrysler; COO of FCA North America (2011–2018)
NTC	Governed by Joint Activities Board. VP of Employee Relations and International VP of UAW served as Co-Chair of the JAB, which also included other senior officials of FCA and UAW
General Holiefield (deceased)	UAW International Vice President 2006–2014; 2007–14 served on UAW Executive Board
Dennis D. Williams	UAW Secretary-Treasurer 2010–14; International President 2014–2018

(Continued)

Table 10.1 (Cont.)

Norwood H. Jewell	International Vice President 2014–2017; Regional Director (2010–2014); on April 2 2019 Jewell pled guilty to conspiracy to violate the Labor Management Relations Act
Virdell King	Senior official UAW Chrysler Department from 2008 until retirement in February 2016; pled guilty on August 29, 2017 to conspiracy to violate LMRA; sentenced to prison and $5,500 fine
Nancy Johnson	Top Adm. Assistant to Jewell from 2014–2016; pled guilty on conspiracy to violate LMRA; sentenced to one year and one day in prison and $10,000 fine
Keith Mickens	Senior official to UAW Chrysler Department from 2010 through 2015; served as Co-Director of the NTC and on the JAB; pled guilty to conspiracy to violate the LMRA and sentenced to one year, one day in prison and $10,000 fine
Wilson's Diversifed [sic] Products LLC	
Monica Morgan Photography	
Leave the Light on Foundation (LTLOF)	Keith Mickens (VP and Director); Jerome Durden (Treasurer and Director); Virdell King (Director)
Racketeering Enterprises	
FCA-NTC Enterprise	Joint Training Center funded by FCA/Chrysler
FCA-Control Enterprise	(UAW)

In its amended suit filed on August 3, 2020, GM added Dennis Williams and Joseph Ashton as defendants, and identified several other FCA officials as non-parties to the suit. The amended suit alleged that the FCA-led efforts to corrupt the collective bargaining process were more systemic and widespread than originally believed after an independent investigation sponsored by GM to delve deeper into the situation. GM's investigation revealed, as indicated in its amended civil RICO complaint, that FCA had used secret offshore bank accounts to corrupt UAW officials to harm GM by raising its labor costs relative to competitors.[7] The amended complaint stated, in significant part:

> The FCA-NTC Enterprise was operated as an enterprise by Defendants since at least July 2009 for the common purpose of directing funds away from the NTC (and ultimately from FCA Group) and others for the benefit of certain UAW officials in return for benefits, concessions, and advantages to FCA through driving higher labor costs for GM as alleged herein. This purpose was achieved through a variety of related fraudulent schemes. Defendants conducted and participated in the affairs of the

FCA-NTC Enterprise through a pattern of racketeering activity, as defined by 18 U.S.C. § 1961(5), consisting of numerous and repeated uses of the interstate mails, wire communications, and Taft-Hartley violations associated with the NTC, to execute a scheme to defraud in violation of 18 U. S.C. § 1962(c), through violations of 28 U.S.C. § 186, and through violations of 18 U.S.C. § 1956. The NTC was used as a tool to carry out the elements of the illegal schemes and pattern of racketeering of Defendants. The FCA-NTC Enterprise had an ascertainable structure and purposes beyond the scope and commission of the predicate acts and conspiracy to commit such acts. The FCA-NTC Enterprise is separate and distinct from Defendants. The FCA-NTC Enterprise engaged in, and its activities affected, interstate and foreign commerce by, among other things, representing and training workers for national automakers and training workers to participate in an industry that engages in substantial interstate and international trade through its supply chains and systems of distribution. Defendants, through their agents and co-conspirators conducting the affairs of the FCA-NTC Enterprise, had the common purpose to secure funds and directly harm GM to force a merger between GM and FCA as more specifically alleged herein. Defendants, through their agents and co-conspirators, did so by, among other things: illegally manipulating the collective bargaining process, diverting funds from the NTC for the benefit of certain UAW officials, paying bribes by paying double the price of the 2015 CBA, and diverting additional FCA Group funds to involved individuals through the use of foreign bank accounts. Defendants carried out these schemes using the interstate mails and wires in violation of 18 U.S.C. §§ 1341 and 1343 and 29 U.S.C. § 186., among other things, representing and training workers for national automakers and training workers to participate in an industry that engages in substantial interstate and international trade through its supply chains and systems of distribution. Defendants, through their agents and co-conspirators conducting the affairs of the FCA-NTC Enterprise, had the common purpose to secure funds and directly harm GM to force a merger between GM and FCA as more specifically alleged herein. Defendants, through their agents and co-conspirators, did so by, among other things: illegally manipulating the collective bargaining process, diverting funds from the NTC for the benefit of certain UAW officials, paying bribes by paying double the price of the 2015 CBA, and diverting additional FCA Group funds to involved individuals through the use of foreign bank accounts. Defendants carried out these schemes using the interstate mails and wires in violation of 18 U.S.C. §§ 1341 and 1343 and 29 U.S.C. § 186.[8]

The same federal district judge who dismissed the case dismissed the amended case on August 14, 2020, though GM has appealed the case to the

6th Circuit Court of Appeals. GM's suit merits considerable for matters separate from its purely legal qualities because it raises questions about the extent to which the demonstrated bribery, while perhaps not sufficient to warrant a civil RICO prosecution against FCA, may have nonetheless impacted labor-management relations between the parties. A fundamental question also deserves to be raised about the extent to which the financial nexus created between a company and a union through joint training programs funded by the company leads to concern about the parties' institutional independence, which is vital to a free collective bargaining process.

Alleged/Convicted Illegal Conduct

The pattern of racketeering activities revolved around two major sets of schemes: (1) the enrichment of union and corporate officials resulting from an orchestrated attempt to (2) use the FCA/Chrysler National Training Center to influence the UAW in order to extract favorable treatment in the domain of labor-management relations and collective bargaining. We examine the evidence presented by the US Attorney's office and analyze broader implications. In the final analysis, however well intentioned when initially formed, the joint training center became of means by which the corporation could subsidize the UAW in contravention of the intent of labor law to prevent such potential financial dependency. Without question, the UAW-FCA NTC poured millions of dollars into the coffers of the UAW treasury to fund its operations. It also provided the financial base by which to bribe union officials, with select corporate executives also taking advantage of an opportunity to derive personal gain.

Schemes of Bribery and Personal Enrichment

As discussed earlier, the genesis of these interconnected schemes goes back to the very top of Fiat before it affiliated with Chrysler in 2009 as the latter emerged from bankruptcy. CEO Sergio Marchionne, who had led Fiat since 2002, had visions of achieving a merger of historic proportions between Fiat and General Motors dating to the early 2000s. In 2004, as head of Fiat, Marchionne approached the GM leadership with the idea of a combination, which would have made the integrated Fiat-GM the largest auto manufacturer worldwide. In 2005, GM rebuffed Marchionne, who was undeterred despite being unrequited.

The next opportunity for a prospecting a merger came in the midst of the Great Recession, which catapulted the Detroit 3 to the brink of liquidation. Chrysler entered bankruptcy in April 2009, after suffering huge financial losses dues to plummeting sales. In late 2008, it entered into a "Global Strategic Alliance" with Fiat, a European-based company. Marchionne eagerly sought the alliance to use the resuscitation of Chrysler as a stepping stone to position Fiat-Chrysler to merge with GM. In the mid-2000s, Fiat had annual sales of about 2.5 million vehicles compared to Chrysler's 2 million. The alliance called for Fiat to assume on initial 20 percent ownership of Chrysler, with the remainder to be divided between the UAW Retiree Medical Benefit Trust (55 percent) VEBA and the US Government (25 percent). This alliance required approval of the government appointed team charged with restructuring the auto industry to keep the Detroit 3 from going into complete liquidation with the resulting loss of thousands of US jobs.

As Chrysler emerged from bankruptcy in 2010, Fiat assumed 58.5 percent state in the exiting company, with the remaining ownership held by the aforementioned voluntary beneficial employee association, the UAW RMBT VEBA, operating under Trust. To get the new Fiat-Chrysler alliance ready for a possible merger with GM, Marchionne faced two challenges. First, he had to take full ownership of Chrysler from the UAW Trust. As long as the Trust held its stake in the company, the UAW potentially exercised veto power of any prospective merger, which raises the second challenge. Specifically Marchionne had to convince the UAW to persuade the Trust to sell its share of Chrysler. Toward this end, the crafty Fiat/Chrysler CEO allegedly launched a concerted effort to induce UAW cooperation. Outright bribery became the inducement of choice.

The GM complaint against FCA NV, a defendant in the case, lays out the origin of the scheme:

> Beginning in July 2009, acting through its agent Marchionne, FCA NV engaged in a pattern of making and approving payments and the provision of things of value to UAW leaders ... Marchionne himself gave improper things of value to UAW leaders, such as in February 2010, when Marchionne provided a custom-made watch worth several thousand dollars to Holiefield. In addition, Marchionne, as the CEO of FCA NV, and to achieve the ultimate goal of a combination between GM and FCA NV, instructed high-ranking FCA executives, including Iacobelli, to make more than $1.5 million in prohibited payments and things of value directly and indirectly to top UAW officials. Marchionne made these payments, and approved other such payments, within the scope of his employment with and for the benefit of FCA NV. Each of these payments made and approved by Marchionne were in violation of 29 U.S.C. 186 [the Labor Management Relations Act of 1947].[10]

Henceforth, the UAW/FCA NTC morphed into the FCA NTC Enterprise to allegedly bribe UAW officials and infect the union itself with financial transfusions that transposed it into the FCA-Control Enterprise. The ultimate goal being, of course, the corrupting of the collective bargaining and broader labor-management relations processes to improve the financial position of FCA NV, thereby making a more attractive prospect for a GM merger. A parade of scheme-implementing bribes apparently ensued, the source of which (namely, the UAW-FCA NTC) became tempting for certain corporate officials to tap for their own personal gain. *What is good for the goose is good for the gander.*

The UAW-FCA NTC—a.k.a. FCA NTC Enterprise—allegedly became an ad hoc expense account to pay for personal goods and services for select corporate and union officials, with the largesse totaling several million dollars in the period between 2009 and 2016. The principal beneficiaries included the top labor relations executive of FCA, who exploited the scheme motivated to corrupt the UAW for personal gain, and two successive International Vice Presidents of the UAW and a personal associate of one of the UAW officials. They were aided by several other corporate and union officials who facilitated the improper expenditures and also, to a lesser degree, derived some personal benefit.[11]

Table 10.2 lists several of the transactions which comprise the "bribes" channeled to corporate and UAW officials.[12] A substantial portion of the overall amount of bribery went to the late General Holiefield and his then-girlfriend/fiancée/spouse, Monica Morgan-Holiefield. Some of the money was transferred from the NTC to the Leave the Lights on Foundation (LTLOF) headed by Holiefield, with various other FCA and UAW officials participating on the charity's board. The LTLOF subsequently paid Holiefield and Morgan either directly or through companies established by Monica Morgan or Morgan and Holiefield jointly, such as Monica Morgan Photography and Wilson's Diversifed [sic] Products, which in turn paid these two individuals.

The series of alleged bribes reveal that the UAW-FCA NTC channeled, directly or indirectly, over $1.2 million to the personal gain of General Holiefield and his girlfriend/spouse, Monica Morgan. The beneficiaries used these funds to pay for trips, designer clothes, jewelry, and entertainment. In addition, they received funds to pay for closing costs on the purchase of a house and for their mortgage of over $262,000. The UAW-FCA NTC made these donations directly to the parties or through a charity (LTLOF) controlled by Holiefield and companied owned by either Morgan or Holiefield.

While the alleged bribes for the UAW officials started in 2009, Alphons Iacobelli evidently became tempted to partake of the easily available largesse.[14] Through corporate and union officials associated with the UAW-FCA NTC, he arranged to receive over $1.44 million in illegal funds, to pay for various home improvements, personal items, and a 2013 Ferrari worth more than $350,000. It is known that falsified IRS 990 tax forms were filed on behalf of UAW-FCA NTC between 2010 and 2014, with the failure to report over $1.48 million in illegal expenditures that benefited corporate and union officials.

The FCA-Control Enterprise: A Company Union?

The alleged orchestrated scheme of bribery arguably paved the way to achieve the ultimate goal of concessions from the UAW for the corporation's

Table 10.2 Alleged Overt Acts of Illegal Transfers or Bribes Using UAW-FCA NTC Funds[13]

July 2009	UAW-FCA NTC transfers $15,000 to LTLOF
February 2010	Marchionne gives Holiefield a custom-made Terra Cielo Mare watch worth several thousand dollars declaring the watch as less than $50 to avoid a conflict of interest
July 2009–2014	UAW-FCA NTC transferred more than $386,400 funds from NTC to LTLOF
January 2011-July 2012	UAW-FCA NTC transferred to more than $425,000 to Wilson's Diversifed [sic] Products; funds used in part of pay for closing costs of the purchase of a house
2012	UAW-FCA NTC transferred another $200,000-plus to another Monica Morgan shell company, Morgan Company A, located in Detroit, Michigan
May 2011-October 2013	LTLOF transferred over $350,000 to General Holiefield and Monica Morgan for personal use, which involved a "fake hospice" created to receive foundation funds
June 2014	UAW-FCA NTC wire transferred $262,219.71 to pay off Holiefield's mortgage
December 2014–February 2016	Iacobelli, Nancy Johnson, Virdell King, Keith Mickens, Norwood Jewell, and Dennis Williams used tens of thousands of UAW-FCA NTC funds to make personal purchases, including $1,259.17 for luxury luggage; $2,182 for an Italian-made Beretta shotgun; $2,130 for Disney World theme park tickets; $1,000-plus for Christian Louboutin designer shoes; numerous expensive meals costing: $7,579.55; $4,587.04; $3,372.74; $6,200.05; $4,147.74; $6,081.04; $3,583.47 at various Palm Springs, CA restaurants
2010–2014	Jerome Durden filed false IRS 990 forms on behalf of the UAW-FCA NTC failing to identify hundreds of thousands of dollars in transfers: $195,015 in 2010; $543,960 in 2011; $335,852 in 2012; $145,054 in 2013; $262,000 in 2014; these "failures" totaled $1,481,890 over these five years
2012–2014	UAW-FCA NTC transferred $40,684 to complete the purchase of two limited edition solid gold Mont Blanc fountain pens costing $35,700 each by Alphons Iacobelli; transferred $159,425 to pay for Iacobelli's credit card expenses; transferred $375,047 to pay for Iacobelli's swimming pool installation, outdoor kitchen, landscaping, and outdoor spa at various his locations; transferred more than $403,834 to pay for Iacobelli's credit card expenses; transferred more than $350,000 to Iacobelli to purchase a 2013 Ferrari 458 Spider, more than $44,491 to pay for his credit card expenses, and more than $67,500 in personal travel by private jet for himself and others. Altogether these transfers totaled $1,440,981

competitive advantage. GM's complaint accused select FCA corporate officials of seeking preferential treatment in three respects: (1) the introduction of a system of World Class Manufacturing aimed at improving productivity and quality; (2) greater use of Tier Two (lower cost) and temporary (again lower cost) workers relative to GM and Ford; and (3) smoother processing of grievances to improve the labor-management relations climate and reduce the costs of administering grievance procedures. Achieving these objectives would put the Fiat-Chrysler company in a more attractive position to interest GM in a merger.[15]

But the FCA leadership did more than prime the pump with alleged bribes.[16] It also infected the UAW proper, pouring millions of dollars into its treasury from the UAW-FCA NTC, which was funded by the company according the previously mentioned CBAs. While the training center had long provided financial assistance to the union by covering the costs of various union employees assigned to the center, its role became more vital when the UAW experienced serious financial troubles on the heels of the Great Recession, when its membership had plummeted to just above 350,000 (see Table 10.3). Its principal source of revenue, the per capita tax on members (i.e. dues) had fallen from roughly $169 million in 2007 to about $119 million in 2010, while its overall receipts dropped from $328 million to about $274 million in 2010. Thus, its per capita tax revenues fell from over 51 percent of total receipts to just above 43 percent. As shown in Chapter Three, the UAW had to downsize considerably after the Great Recession to adjust to a deteriorating financial situation.

Interestingly, between 2007 and 2018, the UAW-FCA NTC made anywhere from $17.5 million to over $30.6 million per year in "chargeback" payments to the UAW treasury (Table 10.3). These chargebacks covered the compensation of UAW staff assigned to the training center, plus, according to GM's complaint against FCA, a seven percent "administrative tax."[18] For most intents and purposes, the administrative tax amounted to "profit" for the UAW. Regardless, the chargebacks represented a sizable financial subsidy to the union, ranging from about 6.5 percent of total receipts (2010) to nearly 12 percent (2016). The total amount of chargebacks made in any given year climbed significant in absolute terms in 2015 and 2016, which coincided with the negotiation and initial implementation of a contract negotiated by the UAW and the Detroit 3 in the former year. These years also represented Dennis Williams' first two full years at the helm of the UAW, having been elected president at the union's June 2014 convention to succeed Bob King.

The sentencing memorandum the US Attorney's office filed on August 20, 2018 summed up the motivation behind the chargebacks:

> Through this criminal conspiracy to violate the Taft-Hartley Act, FCA, through Iacobelli and its executives, was implementing a corporate policy to buy good relationships with UAW officials. As one FCA executive put

Table 10.3 UAW Per Capita Tax (Member Dues), Total Receipts, and Detroit 3 Joint Training Program Chargebacks, 2007–2013[17]

Year	Per Capita Taxes	Total Receipts	Per Capita Taxes as % of Total Receipts	Chargebacks from Detroit 3 Joint Programs	Chargebacks as % of Total Receipts	Chargebacks as % of Per Capita Taxes
2018	$180,698,171	$256,382,935	70.48%	$ 20,773,478	8.10%	11.50%
2017	$175,761,301	$273,613,195	64.24%	$ 25,633,892	9.37%	14.58%
2016	$182,485,234	$261,207,437	69.86%	$ 30,635,207	11.73%	16.79%
2015	$168,335,253	$289,117,330	58.22%	$ 26,280,330	9.09%	15.61%
2014	$116,785,381	$219,808,402	53.13%	$ 21,876,090	9.95%	18.73%
2013	$115,110,392	$214,010,485	53.79%	$ 21,627,799	10.11%	18.79%
2012	$114,997,341	$261,144,414	44.04%	$ 21,463,562	8.22%	18.66%
2011	$122,377,196	$257,779,290	47.47%	$ 17,570,243	6.82%	14.36%
2010	$118,985,490	$274,044,321	43.42%	$ 17,570,243	6.41%	14.77%
2009	$127,473,363	$277,401,995	45.95%	$ 21,502,459	7.75%	16.87%
2008	$161,302,621	$315,772,004	51.08%	$ 21,775,277	6.90%	13.50%
2007	$168,747,110	$327,637,840	51.50%	$ 28,424,870	8.68%	16.84%

Source: US Department of Labor LM-2 Reports

it, FCA was making an "investment," by "spending thousands here," in the form of illegal payments to UAW officials through the NTC, in an effort to obtain benefits, concessions, and advantages for FCA in its relationship with the UAW. FCA executives sought to keep UAW officials "fat, dumb, and happy" with their few thousand dollars and credit cards, whereas FCA was seeking advantages and concessions in the negotiation and administration of the collective bargaining agreements.[19]

As the sentencing memorandum also noted:

FCA and Iacobelli directed a stream of income of millions of dollars to the UAW as an entity. Ostensibly, FCA reimbursed the UAW for the salaries and benefits of UAW officials who were assigned to and worked at the NTC. This payment of salaries of UAW officials with money provided by the FCA was known as "chargebacks." Some UAW officials actually did work at the NTC ... However, a large number of UAW officials ... actually spend their time doing UAW work ... Iacobelli and FCA viewed the chargebacks to FCA of these UAW salaries as a political gift to the UAW ... It was merely a corrupt mechanism whereby FCA money could be used by the UAW to keep the UAW's costs down.[20]

GM Seeks Relief in the Complaint

In its RICO suit, GM sought relief. Specifically, it wanted (1) damages to cover the, to be determined at trial, billions of dollars of damages GM suffered from FCA's bribery, racketeering, and other unlawful activities; (2) punitive and exemplary damages; (3) recovery of the costs incurred in pursuing this litigation; (4) equitable relief, including restitution; and "Any other relief the Court deems just, fair, necessary, or equitable."[21]

In close, GM's comprehensive suit and the relief it seeks beg the question of the extent to which FCA's patterns of misconduct actually corrupted the collective bargaining and labor-management relations processes to the competitive advantage of the other domestic producers who bargained with the UAW.

Federal Judge Dismisses GM Suit

On July 8, 2020, Federal Judge Paul Borman dismissed GM's RICO suit against FCA.[22] He had earlier ordered the CEOs of the two companies to meet to resolve their differences. The 6th Circuit US Court of Appeals overruled the order, prompting the judge to dismiss the case. A GM spokesperson indicated that the company felt they had sufficient evidence of racketeering to merit the complaint, which implicated institutions and individuals.[23]

As noted, GM filed an amended suit on August 3, 2020. It reported new revelations of wrongdoing brought to light by investigations it conducted in FCA and its interactions with various UAW officials. It has alleged a deeper conspiracy to corrupt the union to the financial advantage of FCA against GM. Among the more startling allegations made is the accusation that the FCA established secret offshore bank accounts in Switzerland, Luxembourg, and the Cayman Islands to in effect "bribe" favors from UAW officials.[24] The same federal district judge who dismissed the original GM complaint dismissed the amended suit on August 14, 2020, viewing the newly presented evidence as "too speculative," but GM has appealed the case to the US Court of Appeals.[25]

Notes

1 RICO Statute, Public Law 91-452 84 Stat. 922; 18 U.S.C. ch. 96.
2 Lawrence and LaReau, *op. cit.*; Snell, Noble, and Howes, *op. cit.*; Lawrence, E. (2020, August 17). GM Presses Ahead with Appeal in Racketeering Suit Against Fiat Chrysler, *Detroit Free Press.*
3 Ibid; GM Amended Civil Complaint, *op. cit.*
4 GM Civil RICO Complaint; Amended Civil Complaint, *op. cit.*
5 Ibid.
6 Ibid.
7 Ibid.
8 Ibid.
9 USA v. Gary Jones, Criminal Complaint, Second Superseding Information, February 27, 2020, Criminal No. 19–20726, United States District Court Eastern District, Southern Division; USA v. Vance Pearson, Criminal Complaint, September 12, 2019, Case No. 2: 19-mj-30488, United States District Court Eastern District, Southern Division; USA v. Eugene N. Robinson, Plea Bargain, March 2, 2020, Case No. 19-cr-20726, United States District Court Eastern District Michigan, Southern Division; GM LLC, General Motors Company v. FCA, Alphons Iacobelli, Michael Durden, and Michael Brown, Civil Complaint, November 20, 2019, Case 2: 19-cv-13429, United States District Court Eastern District, Southern Division; GM LLC v. FCA, Dennis Williams, Joseph Ashton, Alphons Iacobelli, Jerome Durden, Michael Brown, First Amended Complaint, Demand for Jury Trial, August 3, 2020, No. 19-cr-13429, United States District Court Eastern District Michigan, Southern Division.
10 GM Civil RICO Complaint; Amended Civil Complaint, *op. cit.*
11 Ibid.
12 Iacobelli, Sentencing Memorandum; Indictment; Plea Bargain; Sentencing Hearing, *op. cit.*; GM Amended Civil Complaint, *op. cit.*
13 USA v. Gary Jones, Criminal Complaint, Second Superseding Information, February 27, 2020, Criminal No. 19–20726, United States District Court Eastern District, Southern Division; USA v. Vance Pearson, Criminal Complaint, September 12, 2019, Case No. 2: 19-mj-30488, United States District Court Eastern District, Southern Division; USA v. Eugene N. Robinson, Plea Bargain, March 2, 2020, Case No. 19-cr-20726, United States District Court Eastern District Michigan, Southern Division; GM LLC, General Motors Company v. FCA, Alphons Iacobelli, Michael Durden, and Michael Brown, Civil Complaint, November 20, 2019, Case 2: 19-cv-13429, United States District Court Eastern District, Southern Division; GM LLC v. FCA, Dennis Williams, Joseph Ashton,

Alphons Iacobelli, Jerome Durden, Michael Brown, First Amended Complaint, Demand for Jury Trial, August 3, 2020, No. 19-cr-13429, United States District Court Eastern District Michigan, Southern Division.

14 Iacobelli, Sentencing Memorandum; Indictment; Plea Bargain; Sentencing Hearing, *op. cit.*; GM Amended Civil Complaint, *op. cit.*

15 Ibid.

16 Brown, Plea Bargain, *op. cit.*; Mickens, Plea Bargain, *op. cit.*; Durden, Plea Bargain, *op. cit.*; GM Amended Civil Complaint, *op. cit.*; Iacobelli, Indictment, *op. cit.*

17 US Department of Labor LM-2 Reports.

18 Brown, Plea Bargain, *op. cit.*

19 Iacobelli, Sentencing Hearing, *op. cit.*

20 Ibid.

21 GM Civil RICO Complaint, *op. cit.*; GM Amended Civil Complaint, *op. cit.*

22 Lawrence and LaReau, *op. cit.*

23 Ibid.

24 GM Amended Civil Complaint, *op. cit.*

25 Snell, Robert (2020, August 14), Judge Refuses to Revive GM Racketeering Suit v. FCA, *The Detroit News*; Lawrence, August 17, 2020, *op. cit.*

Chapter 11

Detroit 3 in Comparison
CBAs, Employment, and Financial Performance

While the scandalous behaviors and subsequent revelations of wrongdoing mounted, the UAW and the Detroit 3 negotiated three sets of major contracts post-2009. In 2011, 2015, and 2019, the parties reached agreements on three sets of four-year contracts, which typically become part of a "pattern" in the US auto industry, given the history of labor-management relations. During the 2019 negotiations in particular, as the public and UAW rank-and-file became increasingly aware of the scope of illegal conduct, questions arose as to what impact it might have had on the collective bargaining process. GM's RICO suit against FCA, in which the UAW is implicated, has alleged that the corruption tainted the collective bargaining process and broader sphere of labor-management relations to its financial disadvantage. Allegedly, top leaders of both the FCA and UAW concocted a plan to promote FCA's interests in merging with GM to gain an even greater foothold in the international auto-manufacturing industry. Though such a merger never came about, FCA has since agreed to merge with PSA, which would make the newly combined company the third largest globally in the industry.

Indeed, a comprehensive report on the origin and scope of the multi-faceted UAW-connected scandals by *the Detroit News* (Howes and Snell 2019) has made the case for concern about the broader economic effects of the serial misconduct:

> Fiat Chrysler executives, armed with $12.5 billion in taxpayer funds, started funneling bribes and illegal payments to UAW officials within days of the automaker emerging from bankruptcy in June 2009, The Detroit News has learned, partially squandering a second chance financed by American taxpayers. Prosecutors allege the money was part of a broad attempt by Fiat Chrysler executives to secure labor concessions from the UAW by keeping labor leaders "fat, dumb and happy."
>
> The government's four-year investigation has revealed how labor leaders misused the bailout's historic second chance by embezzling money from worker paychecks, shaking down union contractors and scheming with auto executives. The conspiracy stretched from the

California desert and a union town on the banks of the Missouri River to the woods of Northern Michigan and the Jersey Shore.

"When the UAW goes on strike and the workers are making — I think it was $275 per week ... And what does the leadership get? Bottles of booze worth $1,300. Lavish steak dinners," US Attorney Matthew Schneider, the Justice Department's top prosecutor in Detroit, told The News.

In all, UAW officials and auto executives are accused of misappropriating nearly $34 million since the bailout 10 years ago, according to an analysis by The News. That money includes embezzled member dues and funds siphoned from facilities that train roughly 150,000 of the union's nearly 400,000 members.

The timing of illegal payments within days of attaining control of Chrysler signals the importance Marchionne appeared to place on buying influence within the UAW, one of the nation's largest and most powerful labor unions. When the remnants of Chrysler emerged from bankruptcy, its UAW retiree health care trust owned a majority stake in the Auburn Hills automaker, and a close relationship with the union could buttress Marchionne's hope of one day acquiring GM, sources familiar with the investigation said.

So far, 13 people tied to the UAW and Fiat Chrysler have been charged in federal court, and prosecutors have implicated at least seven others in the conspiracy. Those include Williams, the union's president emeritus, and recently resigned President Gary Jones, who is accused of stealing as much as $700,000 from workers and trying to cover up crimes. William's attorneys did not respond to requests for comment, and Jones' attorney declined comment.[1]

More specifically, GM has argued in its RICO suit that FCA executives, led by the late CEO Sergio Marchionne, attempted to "buy" the cooperation of UAW officials to effect cost-savings measures that would make FCA a more attractive partner for a merger with the UAW.[2] Indeed, it is alleged that Dennis Williams, the former head of the UAW, eventually became a proponent of the pursued merger and tried to convince a resistance GM leadership to change its opposition. The alleged plan as it pertained to establishing a more competitive labor cost structure involved securing the cooperation of the UAW to introduce the World Class Manufacturing system at the former Chrysler plants, increasing the use of Tier 2 and temporary workers, and smoothing day-to-day labor-management frictions.[3]

In 2009, several major developments had unfolded to reposition the Detroit 3 to recover from the depths of crushing economic downturn and other adverse factors impinging on domestic auto producers. Infused with large amounts of cash from either the federal government (in the case of GM and Chrysler) or bank loans (Ford), the companies had avoided liquidation. But, to reduce overcapacity and excessive employment, the companies closed plants and laid off workers, decreasing hourly employment by more than 50,000 between 2007 and 2009.[4] Comparably steep reductions occurred among salaried workers. The companies also trimmed product lines to align with more profitable segments of their businesses. In addition, Fiat took a larger share of ownership in Chrysler, acquiring 58.5 percent of its assets.

As the new Chrysler and new GM emerged from bankruptcy, they renegotiated their contracts with the UAW. Ford did as well in order to maintain pattern and avoid competitive disadvantage. In this agreement, the parties suspended the cost-of-living-allowances (COLAs) and selected bonuses, suspended "Protected Status" under the Job Security Program (so-called Jobs Bank), and lifted the cap on Tier 2 workers. Even after having made arduous decisions and painful cutbacks, the Detroit 3 faced an uncertain future, with a lot depending on uncontrollable forces, such as the price of oil, consumer preferences, and the state of the global economy. Maintaining a stable labor-management climate became central to the recovery. Toward this specific objective, as a condition for receiving governmental assistance, the UAW had consented to a no-strike pledge. Ford had attempted to secure a similar promise in its 2009 round of UAW negotiations, but rank-and-file rejected a tentative agreement with this proviso, forcing its ultimate abandonment. Yet, each of the companies knew that a strike in the near future would have perhaps irreversibly damaging economic consequences and serious political ramifications, particularly in the case of the new Chrysler and new GM.

The 2011 Negotiations

By 2009–2010, the three companies, including the FCA, by then in a full alliance with Chrysler, had regained profitability by increasing their sales significantly from the depths of the Great Recession while having cut their labor and other costs, which involved making substantial reductions in production capacity.[5] However, the overall sales market for these companies did not rise to level of pre-recession heights as the US market has seemed to have plateaued in the 17-million range of annual motor vehicle sales.

In 2011, the companies and the UAW had to renegotiate their respective four-year contracts. While they had avoided collapse, they still faced relentless international competition, as their collective market share in the US had fallen below 50 percent. In addition, compared to transplants, the Detroit 3 had sizable labor cost disadvantages relative to the transplants (see Table 11.1). Ford and GM had an $8 and $6 per hour gap in total labor costs, respectively, compared to the foreign-owned US-located manufacturers. FCA had a $2 disadvantage. Parenthetically, if FCA were to make itself more competitive on this dimension, it would have to shave its relative costs.

Table 11.1 Total Labor Costs per Hour, Detroit 3 and Transplants[6]

Company	2011	2015	2019
FCA	$52	$47	$55
Ford	$58	$57	$61
GM	$56	$58	$63
Average of Transplants	$50	$47	$50

Source: Automotive News

As the Detroit 3 entered the 2011 negotiations, they had relatively few temporary workers. FCA had less than one percent of its hourly workforce as temps, while GM had two percent with Ford at five percent. In contrast, by 2019, FCA had 13 percent of its workforce as temps, with GM at seven percent and Ford at six percent. The foreign-owned auto plants in the US had 20 percent as temps in 2019.

While the contract negotiations in 2011 involved challenging issues, the parties operated under considerable economic and political pressure to avoid confrontations that would jeopardize their fragile recoveries. After weeks of intense negotiations, each of the Detroit 3 reached agreements with the UAW, once again establishing a general pattern with some company-specific modifications. As show in Table 11.2, the parties agreed to maintain the two-tier wage structure, but rose the base by a slight amount at the second tier. Base wages at Tier 1, or among legacy (pre-2007 hires) were frozen for the life of the contracts (four years), but seniority workers with more than one year of seniority were given ratification bonuses, ranging between $1,750 and $6,000 across the three companies. Each company made significant commitments of new investments to create new jobs. No significant cost shifting occurred in health care. Profit-sharing formulae were changed to be based on earnings before interest and taxes.

Overall, the Detroit 3 generated more than $65 billion in net income in 2011–2014. Their total sales grew pronouncedly since the nadir in 2009, which enabled them to add more hourly workers. One of the biggest sore points that festered in these years was disgruntlement over the Two-Tier wage structure. It created considerable friction among rank-and-file and eroded confidence in the union's capacity to champion solidarity. In addition to having a lower base wage, the second-tier workers lacked a defined benefit pension plan, having instead the defined contribution variety. As the 2015 negotiations drew near, there were demands for collapsing the wage differential and also providing a general wage increase grew.

A couple of interesting developments occurred in the 2011–2015 interim regarding the differentials in the companies' total labor costs and, relatedly, the composition of their workforces. As shown above in Table 11.1, the labor cost differential grew significantly between Ford and GM, on the one

Table 11.2 Key Contract Provisions 2011 and 2015[7]

Item		2011	2015
Base Wage	FCA	No change	Two 3 % increases
	Ford	No change	Two 3 % increases
	GM	No change	Two 3 % increases
Tier 2	FCA	$15.78–$19.28	$15.78–$19.28; 8 year progression
	Ford	$15.78–$19.28	$15.78–$19.28; 8 year progression
	GM	$15.78–$19.28	$15.78–$19.28;8 year progression
COLA	FCA	None	None
	Ford	None	None
	GM	None	None
Jobs	FCA	2,100 new	$5.3 billion in new investment
	Ford	5,750 new	8,500 new or retained jobs; $9 billion in product commitments
	GM	6,400 new	3,300 new or retained; 1.9 billion in new investments
Signing Bonus	FCA	3,500 (1,750 in 2011)	$4,000 seniority employees; $3,000 temps
	Ford	6000 (5000 less than 1 year seniority)	$8,500
	GM	5,000	$8,000 for all employees; $2,000 for temps with 90 days prior to effective date
Profit Sharing	FCA	$1,000/$1b; 85 % worldwide profit; $12,000 cap	Profit-sharing cap removed; formula changed to $800 per 1% NA profit
	Ford	$1,000/$1b NA profit; $12,000 cap	Profit-sharing cap removed, formula retained
	GM	$1,000/$1b NA; $12,000 cap	Profit-sharing formula maintained
Health Care	FCA	No change in worker contribution; $20 co-pay	No cost shifting;
	Ford	No change in worker contribution; $20 co-pay	Traditional health care for in-progression employees
	GM	No change in worker contribution; $25 co-pay	Traditional health care provided for in-progression employees and health care program for temps

(Continued)

Table 11.2 (Cont.)

Item	2011		2015
Other Lump Sums	FCA	$1,000–$2,000 for four years	Two 4 % lump sum payments; 4 $1,000 for eligible workers; 4 $500 Quality Performance Payments
	Ford	$1,750 for four years	Two 4 year lump sum payment
	GM	$1,250 for three years	Two 4 % lump sums; $1,500 yearly inflation protection; $1,500 profit-sharing pre-payment; $250 yearly competitiveness bonus
Traditional Pension/Health Care	FCA	No change in traditional pensions; health care VEBA to receive 10 % of profit sharing	No change in traditional pensions; employer contributions to 401(k) increased from 4 to 6.4 %
	Ford	No change in traditional pensions; health care VEBA to receive 10 % of profit sharing	No change in traditional pensions; employer contributions to in-progression 401(k) increased
	GM	No change in traditional pensions; health care VEBA to receive 10 % of profit sharing	No change in traditional pensions;

hand, and the FCA and transplants, on the other. By 2015, FCA had closed the gap with the transplants, having lowered its costs from $52 per hour to just $47, representing a $5 drop compared to the transplants' $3 reduction. Ford's total labor costs dropped one dollar while GM's rose two. Thus, GM and Ford each had at least a 21 percent disadvantage in labor costs than FCA and the transplants.

One of the reasons for this rising differential rested in escalating use of Tier 2 workers at FCA compared to GM and Ford. By 2015, in violation of the contractual agreement reached in 2009 to cap the percentage of such workers at 25 by that year, FCA had let its lower-tier climb to 45 percent of the total workforce. In contrast, GM's stood at 20 percent and Ford's at 29 percent. FCA had also allowed its temporary workforce to rise proportionately much more than the other two Detroit rivals.

A ritualistic practice associated with "pattern" bargaining in the US auto industry involved the UAW's selecting a "target" company among the Detroit 3 to lead the negotiations. The companies' contracts expired on the same date, but the UAW essentially effected a serial bargaining process, in which the target company would lead the series, following sequentially by the two other companies. It became a popular guessing game among the media and auto observers to speculate on which company would be chosen as the target. In general, the target was selected because it was deemed to facilitate setting the best "pattern" for the auto workers.

The UAW surprised most in 2015 by selecting FCA as its target. For various economic reasons, Fiat Chrysler Automobiles was deemed by industry analysts the weakest to negotiate a strongly pro-worker pattern. Nonetheless, negotiations started at FCA and proceeded slowly at first, when the then-CEO Marchionne and UAW president Williams stepped into bargaining to accelerate the process. On September 15, 2015, the day the contract was set to expire, the parties reached a tentative agreement. This initial tentative agreement, however, proved instantaneously disappointing to rank-and-file, who unloaded their objections with alacrity and vociferousness through social media. The FCA workers eventually voted by 65 percent to reject the contract, which sent the parties back to the bargaining table:

> UAW members rejected a tentative agreement between with Fiat Chrysler by 65% after a ballot on Tuesday, the results of which were finalized on Thursday.
>
> UAW members at large assembly plants in Toledo, Ohio, and Sterling Heights, Michigan, all rejected the pact as did most other factories, by a wide margin.
>
> "We will gather the issues together; notify FCA [Fiat Chrysler] that further discussions are needed. We don't consider this a setback; we consider the membership vote a part of the process we respect," Dennis Williams, president of the UAW, said in a statement.[8]

The principal objection centered on the two-tier wage structure. Opponents of the tentative agreement objected that the Tier 2 workforce would not be shrunk to the 25 percent cap presumed to take effect at that time and that the wage gap would not be fully closed but fall short of the $28 per hour goal at the designated rate of slightly above $25 per hour. UAW leaders knew that they had done a poor job of preparing the rank-and-file to accept the initial results and were caught off guard by the swiftly negative response via social media. Accordingly, as the union leadership went back to table to get a better deal, the UAW also hired a social media consulting firm to help it get its message out better to the rank-and-file when another tentative agreement was reached.

The UAW and FCA did reach a new agreement in mid-October, which included several improvements from the workers' side. As shown in Table 11.2, the FCA-UAW contract that was finally approved by the rank-and-file in October included an eight-year pathway to close the gap between the two tiers.

It retained the two three-percent general wage increases and two four-percent lump sum payments, as initially negotiated. The parties also kept the improvement in the profit-sharing arrangement, which provided for the payouts to be based on 100 percent of North American profits as opposed to 85 percent in the 2011 accord. FCA and the UAW retained their earlier commitment to raise the company's contribution to the Tier 2 worker's 401 (k) plans from 4 to 6.4 percent. To sweeten the deal for FCA's hourly workers, the renegotiated accord increased the ratification or signing bonus from the original $3,000 for more senior workers to $4,000, but the workers did not succeed in imposing the 25 percent cap on Tier 2 workers. [The fact that the FCA did not abide by the earlier commitment to limit the Tier 2 workforce to this cap has led to suspicion that the parties colluded as part of a scandal-cemented pact.]

The ratification of the second FCA tentative agreement paved the way for negotiations to proceed with the other two Detroit 3. Negotiations moved to GM immediately afterwards and then to Ford. These companies followed the pattern, providing for the collapsing of the two-tier wages within eight years, including lump sum and general wage increases of four and three percent, respectively, and maintaining health care benefits without additional cost shifting. GM followed FCA and eliminated the cap on profit-sharing payouts, though Ford did not. GM and Ford also provided for health care for Tier 2 workers, and Ford followed FCA's lead in raising its contributions to the Tier 2 workers' 401(k) plans.

The 2015 agreements proved relatively cash-rich for the rank-and-file. The lump sum payments and wage increases, coupled with the ratification bonuses, put a lot of money into workers' pockets. The profit-sharing formulae allowed for even greater payouts as long as the companies remained profitable. Generally speaking, the companies stayed on profitable paths attained following the bankruptcies. This led to sizable payouts to rank-and-file between 2015 and 2018. For example, between 2015 and 2018, GM paid out an average of $44,700 per worker while Ford paid out $32,700 and FCA $17,250. Ironically, the companies' abilities to make profit-sharing payments raised pressures to make additional improvements in the economic lot of workers as the 2019 contract negotiations neared.

When the 2019 contract negotiations kicked off in July, with the ritualistic face-offs between the UAW bargaining teams and their company counterparts, the tone differed sharply from the amicability shown in 2015. Despite profitability, Ford and GM had announced significant downsizing in 2018. GM had announced plan to shutter five plants, four in the US and one in Canada. Auto sales had declined and the industry was buffeted by disruptive technological changes. The 2019 kickoffs appeared far more confrontational in tone that the preceding ones in 2015, raising speculation of an inevitable strike.[9]

The shift in attitudes between these two sets of negotiations reflected not only changing developments in the industry, which raised questions and doubts about the future, but also the mounting revelations of scandalous activities as the highest levels of the UAW. Various observers speculated about how these revelations, and whatever truths that might lie behind them, might affect bargaining. UAW officialdom had maintained that the scandals had not tainted bargaining, though these denials did not obviate reservations. Daniel Howes (2019) speculated the UAW-FCA scandal represented a cloud hanging over the upcoming negotiations:

> Detroit's national contract talks traditionally featured two sides at the negotiating table — the United Auto Workers and the "target" company, which this year is General Motors Co.
>
> Not anymore. Not with the Justice Department, the FBI, the Internal Revenue Service and the Labor Department widening their years-long probe into corruption at Solidarity House and in joint training centers funded by the automakers. Not after law-enforcement raids approved by federal magistrate judges in four states last week searched the homes of UAW President Gary Jones and his predecessor, Dennis Williams.[10]

Against this background, the UAW announced in early September 2020 that General Motors was its target company.

As the parties neared the formal commencement of bargaining in September, with the contracts due to expire and the end of the day on September 14, 2019, the issues in dispute focused. The UAW wanted to forestall future job losses, particularly those that might involve a further shift in production to Mexico, where wages among the auto manufacturers averaged less than $8 per hour. It wanted a speedier path to close the gap between the tiered wages, maintenance of the gold standard in health care benefits, which were costing GM over $1 billion per year for its current workforce. Another significant issue to emerge concerned the rising use of temporary workers. As noted, the percentage of temp hourly workers had risen to 13 percent at FCA and between 6–7 percent at Ford and GM. The Tier 2 in-progression workforce, to make matters more challenging from a bargaining perspective, had climbed to almost 60 percent at FCA. At GM and Ford, it stood at 41 and 34 percent, respectively. Each company had workforce splintered in terms of level of base pay and overall compensation, including benefits. Temporary workers did not have full health care benefits, nor did they have access to retirement packages. The UAW negotiators claimed that these so-called temporary workers were often being retained for extended periods of time, in lieu of hiring the more expensive "permanent" workers, who would be paid more with better benefits.

The UAW announced on September 13, 2019 that it was "targeting" GM, which had provoked the most animosity among rank-and-file because of its earlier announced plant closures. The negotiations started slowly, against of backdrop of rising speculation about an "inevitable" strike. UAW members had authorized a strike a few days before the contract expiration. Such votes often have the appearance of being symbolic formalities, but in 2019 they received more serious notice. The UAW had primed the rank-and-file to prepare for strike, having raised its dues in 2014 to shore up its then dwindling strike fund. The companies, also in anticipation of a strike, had built inventories to give them a cushion in case of a disruption in production due to a strike.

As the Detroit 3 contracts expired on September 15, 2019, UAW workers for a GM contractor, Aramark, which supplied custodial services, went out on strike with the coterminous expiration of their own contract. Top UAW leadership convened a meeting of local union presidents representing GM rank-and-file for September 16, 2019, to vote on whether to strike. A strike was called to begin at midnight of September 17, 2019 unless a tentative agreement were within grasp. At that time, lacking an agreement, the UAW workers at GM struck, joining their Aramark brothers and sisters on the picket lines. A prolonged strike ensued, lasting 40 days, making it one of the longest in UAW history. It involved roughly 48,000 UAW members at 34 GM plants. The strike had negative rippling effects, resulting in the layoff of tens of thousands of more workers for adversely affect automobile suppliers. The 40-day strike cost GM a reported $3 billion.

To get a deal, GM had to make significant cash payouts, which were followed at Ford and FCA in more or less rapid succession (see Table 11.3). The parties expedited the path to closing the tiered wage gaps, established a path for temporary workers to earn permanent status, offered a health care plan to temps, preserved health care benefits, procured sizable product investments ($7.7 billion in the case of GM), granted general wage increases and lump sum payments, continued profit sharing, and paid hefty ratification bonuses.

Dissolution of the Joint Training Centers

During these negotiations, the issue of the joint training programs came up in each case, probably due to the federal investigations and negative media attention. Across the three contractual settlements, the parties agreed to dissolve the existing training programs. Each agreement provided that the existing program would be replaced with two separate trust funds allowable under section 302 of the LMRA: (1) a Labor-Management Committees Trust Fund [to be established as an IRS Section 501(c)(5)]; and (2) Voluntary Employees' Beneficiary Association (VEBA) Trust Fund [an IRS 501(c)(9), or 501(c)(5) in the case of GM]. Before these Trust Funds become operational, the contracts provide for a transition period in which the current programs would be phased into termination. In the FCA and GM contracts, the parties stipulated that their existing program buildings would be sold. Ford's contract did not specify what would be done with the NPC building.

Table 11.3 2019 UAW Contract Provisions with Detroit 3.[11]

Item	FCA	FORD	GM
Jobs/Product	7,900 new jobs; $9 billion total investment ($4.5 billion new)	Over $6 billion to create or retain over 8,500 jobs; moratorium on outsourcing and plant closures, except for Romeo Engine	$7.7 billion committed for 5,400 new or retained jobs
General Wage Increases	Two 3% increases; two 4% lump sums	Two 3% increases; two 4% lump sums	Two 3% increases; two 4% lump sums
Tiers—In-progression	All full-time employees at top rate in four years	Temporary workers are eligible to become full-time seniority employees with potential to reach to rate during life of contract; all in-progression employees will grow to parity in life of contract	Paths set for full-time and part-time temps to achieve permanent status; all in-progression to reach $32.32 within four years
Ratification Bonus	$9,000 for qualified seniority; $3,500 for temps	$9,000 for qualified seniority; $3,500 for temps	$11,000 for qualified seniority; $4,500 for temps
Other Bonuses	$500 performance bonus to eligible seniority employees; $1000 quality achievement for eligible seniority employees	$1,500 inflation protection for three years	
Profit Sharing	$12,000 cap removed; formula increased from $800 per 1% of profit to $900	Profit-sharing formula maintained of $1,000 per 1%	Cap of $12,000 lifted and formula of $1,000 per 1% maintained
Health Care	Health insurance for all in-progression employees; no cost shifting to employees	No cost shifting nor reduction in benefits	No cost shifting nor reduction in benefits
Holidays	Additional paid holiday for July 3, 2023	Additional paid holiday for July 3, 2023	Additional paid holiday for July 3, 2023

(Continued)

Table 11.3 (Cont.)

Item	FCA	FORD	GM
Pension	Increased participation rate to 3% on 401(K) and no limit on deferred compensation for savings plan	$1,000 one-time contribution to savings plan for employees hired or rehired before 2007	$1,000 one-time contribution to savings plan for employees hired before 2007
Retirement Bonus	$60,000 for eligible workers	$60,000 for all production employees and up to 200 skilled trades workers	$60,000 for 2,000 eligible production and 60 eligible skilled workers

The contracts specify that the Trust Funds would be operated according to strict financial controls. Funds may not be spent non-programmatic purposes. FCA's agreement with the UAW including illustrative language these types of strictures:

1   The assets of the Trust Funds will be used for the exclusive benefit of Joint Activities and other programs as set forth herein, and to defray reasonable and necessary costs of such programs, including the NTC's wind down costs, legal fees and expenses, and any carry-over obligations of the NTC in accordance with applicable law, and for no other purpose including charitable or other non-program activities.
2   The joint purchase, sale or distribution of FCA-UAW promotional products and novelty items shall be prohibited.
3   The Company shall have the right to review all proposed expenditures of the Trustees of the respective Trust Funds and to accept, modify, or reject those expenditures in the sole and exclusive discretion of the Company. The Company is responsible for establishing internal controls for the Trust Funds and such Trust Funds will be audited on an annual basis by an external independent public accounting firm.[12]

These Trust Funds will be used to provide for education and training in such areas, at FCA, as World Class Manufacturing, product quality and job security, diversity and inclusion, workplace behavior, health and safety, and new hire orientation.

Notes

1   Howes and Snell, *op. cit.*; https://uawinvestigation.com/.
2   GM Civil RICO Complaint, *op. cit.*; GM Amended Civil Complaint, *op. cit.*
3   Ibid.

4 Canis et al., *op. cit.* Canis and Yacubucci, *op. cit.*; McAlinden, *op. cit.*; Schwartz, *op. cit.*
5 Canis et al., *op. cit.*
6 http://www.cargroup.org/wp-content/uploads/2017/02/2011-Detroit-3_UAW-Labor-Contract-Negotiations.pdf; https://uaw.org/see-summary-tentative-agreement-gm/; https://uaw.org/wp-content/uploads/2019/12/56461-UAW-Hourly_rev3.pdf; https://uaw.org/uaw-auto-bargaining/fordcontract/; https://uaw.org/uaw-auto-bargaining/fca-us/; https://uaw.org/wp-content/uploads/2015/11/reducedFINAL-FORD-HOURLY-11-9-15-1229p-FINAL-with-numbers-p24-headings-page-6-charts-p25.pdf; https://uaw.org/contractsummary/; https://uaw.org/fordhighlighter/; https://uaw.org/uaw-auto-bargaining/; Ford Motor Company, 2015 , *op. cit.*; Ford Motor Company, 2019, *op. cit.*
7 GM Amended Civil Complaint, *op. cit.*
8 Howes, D. (2019, September 4). Probe Looms Over UAW-GM Talks, *The Detroit News;* Howes and Snell, *op. cit.*
9 Ibid.
10 Ibid.
11 https://uaw.org/contractsummary/; https://uaw.org/fordhighlighter/; https://uaw.org/uaw-auto-bargaining/
12 Howes, *op. cit.;* Howes and Snell, *op. cit.*

Chapter 12

Reforming the UAW

The revelations of wrongdoing and consequent prosecutorial actions have produced various efforts to reform the UAW in order to prevent recurring incidents. Three successive UAW International Presidents (ironically including two implicated in the scandal) have introduced reforms for such purpose. Unite All Workers for Democracy (UAWD), a grassroots movement within the union, has initiated a call for a special constitutional convention to adopt broader changes such as the direct election of members of the UAW's IEB.[1] Others, including the US Attorney prosecuting the case, have suggested that the federal government may consider taking over the union. The government's takeover of the IBT in the late 1980s has provided prominent precedent for such action.[2]

A fundamental question in assessing alternative remedies lies in what effect they might have in terms of mitigating the chances of such criminal and unethical conduct from occurring the first place. In this regard, it merits note that criminal activity precedes legal enforcement. Similarly, unethical conduct precedes the invocation of ethical codes. In and of themselves, laws and codes cannot completely prevent improper conduct. However, the penalties associated with violations may serve to deter misconduct. In addition, if additional measures are taken to control and audit financial practices, they may further discourage overt acts of noncompliance. Thus, organizational policies and practices which promote financial transparency and auditory oversight might prove important deterrents.

A genuinely prophylactic measure, however, requires ensuring the union and corporate officers possess the desirable ethics before assuming office and continue this frame of conduct once in power. [Beware of the truism: Power corrupts and absolute power corrupts absolutely.] Accordingly, it becomes important to look at how organizations choose their leaders and then go about staffing the organization. We focus here on relevant practice in the UAW, leaving aside how corporations select officers, even though the UAW scandal implicated several FCA officials. In the case of unions, which occupy a special place institutionally in the framework of labor law and labor-management relations, the process of selecting leaders is established through their duly enacted constitutional procedures. The LMRDA provides a "Bill of Rights" for rank-and-file to participate in the selection of officers at all hierarchical levels, including the national or international.[3] The specific election procedures adopted by a union, however, may vary within the legal framework. Thus, a union may choose its international officers by constitutional convention, with elected delegates choosing these officials, or by direct secret ballot election of the rank-and-file. Direct elections may occur by mail or require on-site voting. Most unions choose international officers by convention, though several, such as the United Steelworkers and IBT, use the direct vote method. Conventional wisdom holds that direct, secret ballot elections foster a more democratic union, which some argue is a vital precondition to ridding a labor organization of tendencies to become corrupt.[4] However, when unions choose their international officers by convention, they raise the importance of electoral competition in electing delegates. Historically, while the UAW is noted for its one-party rule under the Administrative Caucus, its elections for convention delegates have generally been relatively competitive.[5]

We address these matters. Specifically, we review the variety of misconduct and the multiple ways in which it violated existing laws and ethical codes. This depiction provides a benchmark against which to compare the sets of reforms that the UAW leadership has promulgated since 2017. Our analysis focuses on the adequacy of proposed reforms as deterrents to future misconduct. It also examines how to draw the boundaries between business and labor in their efforts to solve problems through joint programs. Furthermore, the issues involved in a government takeover are discussed, based on an assessment of experience with the case of the IBT's consent decree that provided for extensive government intervention and control.

Pre-Scandal Ethical and Legal Standards

The numerous indictments and convictions obtained by the US Attorney in the UAW scandal, coupled with efforts to oust officials within the union and to reform itself and the emergence of a grassroots movement to force change on a leadership indebted to the Administrative Caucus, testify to the value of the legal and ethical sanctions that were in place to punishing the wrongdoers. At that time, labor laws and selected other statutes made it illegal for union (and corporate) officers to commit acts of bribery, extortion, embezzlement, theft, fraud, the filing of false reports, the use of interstate commerce to commit crimes, fiduciary malfeasance, and racketeering. The UAW's Ethical Practices Codes added another layer of sanctions, which could be used to impose penalties such as removal from office or expulsion from the union. Though laws and codes proscribing certain conduct serve as a potential deterrent, their use as prosecutorial tools is inherently reactive. The resulting prosecutions bespeak the failure of law and regulation as a deterrent.

Table 12.1 portrays the gamut of criminal, unethical, and problematic conduct along with the then-available legal and ethical codes to punish wrongdoing. The misconduct uncovered by prosecutors falls into five principal categories: bribery and extortion; embezzlement and theft; fraud and falsification of reports; failure to uphold fiduciary duties; racketeering. These overt acts clearly violate extant law, and there can be little doubt in the minds of perpetrators of their illegality. We add a sixth category of activities which may appear less clear-cut in terms of legality but at the same time are of potentially greater import from an institutional standpoint. These activities revolve around the Detroit 3's financial subsidization of the UAW to support union personnel assigned to the joint training centers. Funded by the companies, the joint training centers transferred funds to the union, as previously noted, to "reimburse" the UAW for assigned staff. Such subsidization raises questions about the institutional integrity of the union, to the extent it is deriving financial gain from the companies, albeit through joint training units. It becomes even more problematic when the subsidies compensate "ghost employees" who are nominally assigned by the union to work for the training programs but in fact do no such work.

Given that the force of law and ethics clearly banned the financial misconduct for which the perpetrators have been indicted and convicted, the obvious question becomes why they failed as deterrents. An equally clear answer lies in human nature. Simply put, greed and power motivate misconduct, encouraging people with such an inclination to violate strictures. When it comes to finding ways to cheat the system, as it were, few constraints exist on the potential for human creativity and entrepreneurship beyond one's personal sense of ethics. As mentioned, legal prohibitions and enumerated ethical standards may deter misconduct in some cases, but they are tools used to punish wrongdoing afterwards. Rules *per se* do not erase

Table 12.1 A Typology of Misconduct and Legal/Ethical Applications to the UAW Scandal Preceding Reforms[6]

Misconduct	Legal and Ethical Applications
Bribery and Extortion	NLRA, LMRA, LMRDA Ethical Practices Codes
Embezzlement and Theft	NLRA, LMRA, LMRDA Ethical Practices Codes
Fraud and Falsification	USC. Wire Fraud and Money Laundering
Fiduciary Malpractice	LMRDA Ethical Practices Codes
Racketeering	Racketeering Influenced and Corrupt Organizations
"Company Unionism"	NLRA Ethical Practices Codes

weaknesses which lead people to seek personal gain at the expense of the greater good. Placing people of high integrity in positions of trust becomes the only sure way of preventing wrongdoing, as long as violations of ethical and legal standards are clearly understood and supported. The case of "company unionism," which is raised by financial subsidization, poses a more serious challenge in terms of drawing the line between ethical/legal and unethical/illegal conduct.

In short, national labor laws forbid corporate and union officers from engaging in bribery, embezzlement, theft, and other financial improprieties in connection with union treasuries or labor-management relations, including funds that would be jointly administered. The Ethical Practices Codes of the UAW reinforce these laws.

Various other federal laws prohibit wire and mail fraud, filing false financial reports, and racketeering, which is an umbrella statute encompassing a plethora of crimes. Simply put, the US Attorney does not suffer a paucity of legal bases for prosecuting the wrongdoing that occurred in the UAW scandal. The RICO statute itself brings into the question how the joint training programs were administered to the extent that they may have funded UAW employees assigned to the NTC who did little or no work for the joint training program.[7] Furthermore, specific laws and regulations requiring the disclosure of the finances of the union (LMRDA), the joint training centers, and the charities sponsored by UAW leaders. But without independent and careful auditing and wide disclosure of comprehensive financial reports, it becomes difficult to uncover misconduct hidden behind accounting machinations.

The range of reforms proposed (and to some extent implemented via the governing authorities of the UAW) breaks into two levels. The first revolves around financial practices to serve as additional checks which would prevent or uncover wrongdoing. These practical measures come with added ethical standards and oversight capabilities. A second level concerns more fundamental matters of union governance, which arguably seek to mitigate the forces which led to a "culture of corruption" in the first instance.[8] The prospect of a government takeover could address both levels. In the case of the IBT, the consent decree reached with the US Department of Justice (DOJ) addressed both levels as well as the apparatus for disciplining union officers and members implicated in wrongdoing.

UAW Leadership Reforms

The US Attorney's office in the Eastern District of Michigan began investigating the UAW scandal in 2015, focusing on financial improprieties among union and corporate officials connected with FCA and its UAW-Chrysler NTC. News broke of the investigation on July 26, 2017 when it was reported that federal prosecutors had charged FCA officials with illegal conduct in relation to the operation of the joint training center (NTC), implicating the deceased

International Vice President of the UAW, General Holifield, and the former Vice President of Employee Relations of FCA.[9] Federal prosecutors accused several corporate officials participating in a scheme to bribe union officials to tilt the collective bargaining process in their favor. While the criminal wrongdoing was arguably of the garden-variety type, including bribery and embezzlement, it has far-reaching implications extending to the institutional integrity of the parties in the conduct of their labor-management relations. The misconduct not only represented an abuse of funds but also a threat to the economic well-being of union members whose interests took a backseat to official greed. At the time of this news report, the US Attorney's investigation is still ongoing, with more indictments possible. GM's amended RICO case, on appeal in the federal court system, could produce more evidence of wrongdoing on a wider scale.

The US Attorney released the indictment on July 25, 2017, which was covered in various news outlets.[10] A July 26, 2017 report in the *Detroit Free Press* revealed that:

> The former labor chief for Fiat Chrysler Automobiles, along with the wife of a former UAW vice president, were indicted Wednesday, accused of using company funds intended for worker training to enrich themselves in a scheme that is expected to ensnare more FCA and union officials in what automotive industry experts are calling the most serious corruption case involving the automotive union in decades.[11]

The then-International President of the UAW, Dennis Williams, who has since been implicated in the UAW scandal, issued a statement on the same day of the indictment minimizing the nature and scope of wrongdoing:

> As you may have seen from news reports, Department of Justice (DOJ) recently announced the results of a months-long investigation into alleged illegal activities among certain individuals associated with the UAW-Chrysler National Training Center (NTC).
>
> An indictment was returned alleging that for a period beginning around 2009, former UAW Vice President General Holiefield and former Vice President for Employee Relations for Fiat Chrysler, Alphons Iacobelli conspired to commit illegal and/or unethical activities including the misallocation of NTC funds, the misuse of NTC credit cards and the provision of unlawful or unethical personal benefits.
>
> To be clear, these allegedly misallocated or misused NTC funds were not UAW dues nor were they union funds. These were monies funded by Chrysler pursuant to the collective bargaining agreement.
>
> As your president, I am appalled by the conduct alleged in the indictment, which constitutes a betrayal of trust by a former member of our union.

The UAW has zero tolerance for corruption or wrongdoing of this kind at any level. While the NTC is a separate entity from the UAW that receives no union dues, the fact is that the abuses alleged in the indictment dishonored the union and the values we have upheld for more than 80 years.

The current UAW leadership had absolutely no knowledge of the alleged fraudulent activities detailed by this indictment until they were brought to our attention by the government. We nevertheless take responsibility for not doing more to exert our influence over the governance policies of the NTC, which might have uncovered this corruption sooner.[12]

As reported in the same *Free Press* article, FCA officials expressed their company's lack of awareness at the time its officials and union counterparts perpetrated the crimes:

"FCA US and the UAW were the victims of malfeasance by certain of their respective employees that held roles at the National Training Center (NTC), an independent legal entity," the company said in a statement. "These egregious acts were neither known to nor sanctioned by FCA US."[13]

Despite his response seeking to minimize the cope of criminal misconduct, the UAW's former president nonetheless felt compelled to announce a series of "reforms" to remedy the situation (see Table 12.2). The changes focused on the NTC as opposed to the UAW itself. They included providing for the annual audit of NTC finances, the preparation of annual budgets by NTC departments, hiring a controller, retaining a new legal counsel, imposing additional controls on credit card usage and vendor contracting practices, and banning joint training centers from contributing to union officials; charities. While commendable, these reforms appeared narrowly contoured and otherwise limited. They focused mainly on the training centers and still allowed union officials to establish their own charities and solicit donations from corporate leaders.

During the more than two years after Williams' reforms, in which period the leadership of the UAW changed hands, revelations of a wider and deeper pattern of misconduct across various units of the union continued to mount. Faced with evidence of more widespread misconduct that caught the viewing public by surprise, Williams' successor, Gary Jones, from Region 5, issued another tranche of reforms in March, 2019. Jones' reforms forbade union officials from soliciting employers, vendors, or joint training centers for their own charities but still allowed such charities and did not preclude soliciting individuals associated with companies. They required an independent audit of the training centers by an independent accounting firm, imposed a three-

Table 12.2 UAW Leadership Reforms[14]

Williams' Reforms: July, 2017	Jones' Reforms: March, 2019	Gamble's Reforms November, 2019
These steps include: • Requiring an annual independent audit of the NTC's finances • Hiring a full-time in-house controller • Requiring annual budgets for each program/department and implementing a budget review process. Budgets are approved by the NTC board of directors • Adopting a plan requiring review and approval of credit card statements for payment by two officers and the controller • Formalizing a written credit card policy, including what is/is not permissible • Implementing an interested persons questionnaire and a conflict of interest policy and creating a hotline to report future suspected wrongdoing • Retaining new legal counsel • Requiring all new vendors to be approved by two officers and the controller • Instituting a formal process for vendor procurement • Instituting a ban on all charitable donations from the NTC to any charity run or controlled by a UAW official.	UAW officials and employees who have established their own separate charitable organizations are banned from soliciting contributions of any kind from any employers, vendors or joint training centers. All joint training centers, which are funded with industry money, are required to have an annual financial audit by an independent accounting firm. Installing "stringent financial reporting and oversight" of the National Training Center operated by FCA, which had been the focus of FBI action. Ford and GM centers will be included, too. All UAW vendor deals will be subject to a three-bid process. UAW staff and employee spending and credit card purchases have new review and approval guidelines. No union leader or negotiator is permitted to accept gifts, gratuities, meals, entertainment, or any other thing of monetary value. UAW financials will be certified by an independent accounting firm and submitted to the membership annually in the UAW Solidarity magazine.	• The establishment of an Ethics Ombudsman to receive, review and respond to ethics complaints and allegations. • The creation of the position of Ethics Officer who will not be an employee of the International Union, but rather an external position with the power to investigate allegations, complaints or matters referred to them by the Ethics Ombudsman or the IEB. The UAW is beginning a national search for an Ethics Officer effective immediately. • The introduction of a new policy that will enhance enforcement against those who have been found guilty of misusing funds and our commitment to seek recovery of all misused or misappropriated funds. • The implementation of stringent monetary controls that increase oversight by the UAW Accounting Department. • The banning of all charitable contributions from UAW joint program centers, vendors, or employers to any charities run or controlled by UAW officials.

- The enactment of accountability measures to the Joint Programs, including that purchases of promotional items using joint program funds have been permanently banned and all expenditures will be controlled, monitored, and regularly audited by independent public accounting firms.
- Finally, UAW will set up an Ethics Hotline to encourage those who may have concerns about or want to report potential ethics violations. The hotline will provide members and employees the ability to anonymously and confidentially submit allegations or complaints about potential violations of the UAW's Ethical Code and other relevant policies.

bid requirement before awarding contracts to vendors, required the independent financial audit of UAW finances, forbade union officials from accepting gifts or gratuities of value, and tightened policies on the use of UAW and training center credit cards. These policies thus extended beyond the training centers into the UAW proper.

Both of these UAW International Presidents' plans had obviously lost credibility as evidence of wrongdoing continued to emerge through 2019, resulting on raids by federal agents on each of their homes in August 2019.[15] Shortly thereafter, federal prosecutors filed the racketeering charges against the former director of Region 5, Vance Pearson, and further implicating Jones in illegalities.[16] Pressure built steadily for the union to oust Jones, who resigned as International President in mid-November 2019.[17] The UAW's IEB, however, had earlier voted 7–6 to grant Jones a paid leave in early November.[18] But just a few weeks later, with further evidence of culpability on his part, Jones had to resign his union membership from the UAW. Between Jones's resignation from the UAW's presidency and membership in the union, the newly installed then-acting International President, Rory Gamble, issued another set of reforms on November 13, 2019. President Gamble's reforms established an Ethics Ombudsman, Ethics Officer, and Ethics Hotline to provide avenues to encourage the reporting and investigation of alleged wrongdoing. Since that time, in April 2020, the UAW announced it had appointed the former chair of the National Labor Relations Board, Wilma Liebman, as its new Ethics Officer.[19]

Expulsion of Union Officers.

In addition to implementing these remedies, the UAW has the option of disciplining officers and members for misconduct. Article 30 of the UAW Constitution specifies a procedure for filing charges against and judging the alleged misconduct of International Officers. Charges may be brought by a requisite number of IEB members (which is presently five) or by an officer's local union and the majority of local unions within the region in which the IEB member is located. A detailed procedure for selecting trial jurors to hear the charges brought against the officer(s) is provided. A minimum two-thirds vote to convict the accused is required. A conviction may result in the penalty of removal from office and expulsion from the union: "In case the accused is found guilty, the Trial Committee may, by a majority vote, reprimand the accused or it may, by two-thirds (2/3) vote, suspend or remove the accused from office, or suspend or expel her/him from membership in the International Union." Article 31 of the UAW Constitution has similar provisions to expel a member from the UAW for violations of the Ethical Practices Code.

On November 21, 2019, the UAW IEB unanimously voted to institute Article 30 proceedings against former president Jones and regional director Pearson, urging that they be expelled from union.[20] This action, as noted, effectively forced Jones's resignation from the union. Both Jones and

Pearson resigned their memberships in November 2019. On January 31, 2020, the IEB initiated Article 31 procedures to remove several other UAW officials connected with the overall scandal, including Joseph Ashton, Norwood Jewell, Eugene Robinson, Nancy Adams-Johnson, Jeffrey Pietrzyk, Michael Grimes, Keith Mickens, and Virdell King. [Ashton, Grimes, and Pietrzyk resigned their memberships in February 2020.][21] In announcing this move, International President Gamble stated that:

> Any UAW member who uses their position to break the law or blatantly violates the sacred oath they took to faithfully serve our members will be subject to removal from their post and expulsion from our union ... My administration, and the entire Executive Board, will continue to hold accountable those who commit criminal conduct or serious violations of our Ethical Practices Code. And we will continue to aggressively implement the critical reforms necessary to strengthen our union's financial controls, oversight, and overall accounting system to ensure the type of conduct described in these charges will not reoccur.[22]

A UAW press release noted further "that these officers and staff engaged in serious misconduct in violation of the law and the Ethical Practices Code of the UAW Constitution."[23]

On December 4, 2019, the IEB selected Rory Gamble as the permanent president for the remainder of Jones' term (until June 2022).[24] In that same meeting, the UAW IEB decided that Region 5 would be split and merged with Regions 4 and 8. This merger became effective February 28, 2020.[25]

Grassroots Proposals

As previously mentioned, the UAW Constitution provides two mechanisms to call a Special Convention to address significant union business which cannot or should not await the occurrence of the next regularly scheduled convention, which now operates on a four-year cycle (the next regular Constitutional Convention is in June 2022). First, the IEB, by a 2/3 vote, has the power to call such a convention. Second, union members may mobilize at the grassroots for this ultimate purpose. A three-part set of requirements governs the grassroots process:

- *Petition signatures.* At least 20 percent of the UAW membership, representing 15 local unions in at least five states must sign a petition that makes a specific calling for the convention; the call must specify precisely the reasons for having such a convention and the agenda of business it will address.

- *Union referendum.* If such a valid petition is presented, the UAW will hold a referendum to vote by secret ballot among union members on whether to hold such a special convention.
- *Election of convention delegates.* If a majority of voting members vote for a convention, then the union will follow its regular constitutional procedures to elect delegates, who be assembled at a specified date and location to deliberate the items presented in the call.

The UAWD initiated the process of calling a special convention in late 2019 to amend the UAW constitution in several important respects.[26] While it failed to gain the nearly 80,000 signatures to trigger a referendum by the self-imposed deadline of February 19, 2020, the UAWD has renewed the petition-drive with a new deadline extended into next year.[27] As noted, a key provision of this call is the proposal to provide for the direct secret ballot election of members of the IEB, including the International President and Secretary-Treasurer, by rank-and-file members. The call also proposes to require the publication of the minutes of IEB meetings, which can now only be inspected by union members by a special request at their regional office. It further recommends changing the way the compensation is set for IEB members by disconnecting it from the pay set for International Representatives. The special-convention advocates argue that it presents a conflict of interest for IEB members to tie their pay to International Representatives when the topic of their compensation is subject to negotiation between the International UAW and the union representing the International Representatives, who are also employees of the union with the statutory right to union representation under the National Labor Relations Act. Parenthetically, it appears that the call includes a provision allowing for an open-ended convention, which would permit the delegates to consider a variety of proposals not contemplated specifically in the call itself.

A Government Takeover?

Perhaps the most extreme measure proposed in response to the UAW scandal involves a prospective government takeover of the union. Precedent exists for this option in the federal government's 1989 consent decree with the IBT which required that the US Department of Justice appoint various monitors to investigate and discipline perpetrators of overt acts of racketeering and to revamp and supervisor election procedures.[28] The US Attorney of Southern New York, Rudy Giuliani, led this takeover, having compiled a successful record or prosecuting organized crime figures several prior years.[29] He relied on the criminal and civil provisions of the Racketeer Influenced and Corrupt Organizations Act (RICO) of 1970 to prosecute the case against the IBT.

As previously noted, RICO has four criminal offenses: (1) using funds derived from racketeering to obtain interest in enterprise; (2) obtaining interest in enterprise through racketeering activity; (3) conducting affairs of an enterprise through a pattern of racketeering; and (4) conspiring to violate the above three. It defines an "enterprise" as any corporation, association, or partnership, with a union being a type of association. Racketeering acts (referred to as "predicate offenses") include violations of a long list of federal criminal offenses: murder, arson, fraud, extortion, bribery, theft, drug trafficking. A pattern of racketeering involves at least two such acts within a ten-year period, including previous convictions. While the RICO statute is often used to combat organized crime, its definition of racketeering extends to situations involving union corruption where predicate acts of racketeering are present.

In addition to its criminal-enforcement options, RICO provides two civil remedies. It empowers victims of RICO offenses to sue "enterprises" for triple damages. (This played no role in *US v. IBT* but, as discussed earlier, is at the heart of GM's racketeering suit against FCA). RICO also authorizes the US DOJ to seek injunctive relief against ongoing RICO violations.

Historically, labor has strongly opposed government interference in the regulation of its internal affairs as a general proposition.[30] Even more vociferous opposition arises when the prospect of a government takeover emerges. In this regard, even the dissident faction within the IBT, namely, the Teamsters for a Democratic Union (TDU), opposed a government takeover of the union, notwithstanding its long history of being mob infested.

The lineage of the eventual takeover of the IBT in 1989 dates to preceding efforts to fight organized crime. Given the demonstrable nexus between organized crime and labor unions, this effort led directly to the doorstep of selected unions with mob ties. The IBT stood at the top of the list. As Jacobs (2006) has documented, federal prosecutors had invoked the civil provisions of RICO to secure a government takeover 21 times between 1982 and 2005.[31]

After years of a painstaking investigation, US Attorney Giuliani filed a 113-page civil RICO suit, with two major appending documents: a 105-page memorandum of law and a 72-page statement documenting the charges against the IBT, its general executive board (GEB), and selected members of organized crime.[32] [These accompanying documents, it is important to know, provided guidance to the federal court which eventually assumed supervision of the takeover the IBT—and subsidiary locals for what amounted to more than 30 years.]

A critical aspect of the initiating civil RICO proceedings that would result in the takeover of a union involves remediation. Specifically, a prosecutor may seek to impose certain remedies in order to solve the problem(s) raised in the suit. In considering whether to accept the recommendations of the US Attorney, a federal judge will pay careful attention to the documented wrongdoing in the civil complaint itself and any appended materials.

US Attorney Giuliani requested several remedies in the RICO suit: (1) a preliminary injunction barring organized embers and associates from participating in IBT affairs; (2) a ban on GEB officers from engaging in racketeering acts, associating with organized crime members, or interfering with a court-appointed liaison; (3) the expulsion of IBT officers and members from the union if found to be RICO violators; (4) the appointment of election officers; and (5) a requirement to disgorge monies derived by corrupt officials and members.[33] On March 14, 1989, the federal district court Judge Edelstein issued the order imposing the agreed upon consent decree on the IBT.[34]

The decree required the appointment of an Independent Authority (IA), Investigations Officer (IO), and Elections Officer (EO) to play a heavy role in the administration and governance of the IBT, with a focus on investigating alleged racketeers.[35] It also ordered the IBT to pay the salaries and expenses of these officers and their staff. In addition, after the certification of the IBT's 1991 election results, the union would be responsible for paying the costs and expenses of a newly appointed three-person Internal Review Board (IRB, which would take over the functions performed by the IA and IO).[36] All told the IRB's expenses ran about $3 million per year. The election officer's expenses ran about $10 million each five-year election cycle.[37]

In 1996, the IBT held its second direct election, in which incumbent president Carey was challenged by James Hoffa, Jr. Carey won the election with 52 percent of the vote, but the EO invalidated the result because of charges that the incumbent had misused union funds to finance his reelection campaign.[38] The EO ordered an election rerun for 1998, which Hoffa won easily. The IRB expelled Carey on July 27, 1998. Carey was indicted but acquitted at trial in 2001. The federal government paid for the costs of the 1998 rerun election, which cost over $20 million.[39]

The IBT operated under the consent decree from 1989 through early 2015, when the federal court approved a five-year transition period to end government intervention. During this period (from 1989 through early November 2010), federal monitors brought charges against nearly 700 IBT officials and members associated with 138 locals in 78 cities in 21 states.[40] More than 250 of these officials held local offices of president, secretary-treasurer, and vice president, while 20 officials held office at the International level. Forty percent of the charges involved the misappropriation of unions. In the five-year transition period, the court replaced the IRB with two Independent Disciplinary Officers. It provided for an Independent Election Officer to be appointed by the IBT and paid for by the union. In February 2020, the federal government's role in managing the IBT ended. The IBT had paid $170 million to cover the expenses of the takeover.[41]

Evaluating the Proposed Reforms

The alternative reforms, both proposed and implemented, deserve careful evaluation to assess their relative merits. We propose three criteria by which to assess the value of alternative remedies: scope of coverage; potential to mitigate or prevent; and clarity. In general, any remedy or set of remedies which covers the gamut of improper conduct serves as an effective deterrent, and provides clear guidance appears to be in the right direction. We focus on the reforms introduced by the three successive UAW presidents, the institutional proposals advanced by UAWD proposal to hold direct elections of International Officers, and the possibility of a government takeover (modeled like the IBT consent decree).

The presidential reforms aim largely to reform financial practices and deal with potential conflicts of interest which cover a wide variety of practices (see Table 12.3). They singularly and collectively aim to deter or mitigate future wrongdoing. They provide clearer guidance as to what is permissible or not and how to engage in financial transactions so as to promote accountability and transparency. However, these proposals do not necessarily change the underlying conditions which may have encouraged some to believe that the existing administrative or bureaucratic system would tolerate wrongdoing. Indeed, the fact that the perpetrators of wrongdoing involved leaders invested with the highest levels of power and trust suggests a more deeply rooted problem.

Institutional reforms, on the other hand, could contribute significantly to the mitigation of a repeat of the past if they resulted in fundamental changes in the character of leaders elected and if members participated diligently to hold leaders accountable through strict scrutiny. But they are not a panacea. Some observers believe that union democracy pursued through direct elections will operate as a reliable prophylactic. This argument, however, rests on the assumption that direct elections will foster a more altruistically vigilant rank-and-file and, usually as corollary, a viable two-party system to prevent reemergence of one-party rule such as through the UAW's Administrative Caucus. The experience of the IBT with decades of government control suggests that this optimism is misplaced. As Jacobs and Cooperman have stated:

> The architects of the *US v. IBT* consent decree would have been well advised to consider Lipset, Trow, and Coleman's observations before committing themselves to rank-and-file elections as an antidote to corruption and racketeering. While the IBT's elections have been, for the most part, free and fair [under the consent decree], they continue to disappoint those who believe that a politically energized rank and file will elect insurgents. During the twenty-two-year remedial phase of *US v. IBT*, the union has become steadily more centralized. Like practically all unions, it functions as a one-party organization.[42]

Table 12.3 Evaluative Framework Applied to Proposed Reforms

Reforms	Scope of Coverage	Mitigation/Deterrence Effect	Clarity
Presidential: Tightening financial practices; auditing; additional reporting; proscribes conflict of interest conduct; enhanced internal enforcement; external ethics review	Focused on preventing overt acts of wrongdoing; investigation and prosecution of such wrongdoing	Relies on deterrence effect though restricted practices, disclosure, and follow up review; questions may arise as to the level of resources and intensity committed to enforce these changes	Clarifies procedures and practices proscribes selected conduct raising conflict of interest issues
Institutional: Direct election of union officers; additional protections for democracy within union	Addresses underlying conditions	Relies on changes in union culture through greater democracy to promote ethical conduct; does not provide for addressing enforcement issues	Standing alone does not provide clear guidance beyond known standards of ethical conduct
Government Takeover: IBT model	Included elements of institutional reform and also efforts to investigate and prosecute wrongdoing	The combined effect of both financial practice and institutional reforms, particularly given the strong emphasis on enforcement and compliance and commitment of supportive resources may produce ethical change and mitigate illegal conduct; but in the case of the IBT with the spotty record of election reforms and need for a costly rerun in 1998, these are not guarantees	Extensive resources devoted to investigation and prosecution as well as election reform and monitoring send a clear message, but again may only go so far if leaders are willing to bend the rules

Indeed, the concept of union democracy itself rests on more than a two-party system or elections for International offices which involve more than one viable slate of candidates. Jacobs and Cooperman have made this point unequivocally:

> An important lesson of *US v. IBT* is that it is a mistake to equate union democracy with democratic elections. Union democracy, like democracy

itself, involves more than just free and democratic elections. Democracy includes respect for free speech, equal treatment, due process, minority interests, local autonomy, and opportunities for rank-and-file participation.[43]

We argue that union democracy—or more democracy—is just a first step toward mitigating corruption, but is not a solution. It is arguably a goal worthy of pursuit in and of itself, though not a failsafe protection. Unions may practice democracy to various degrees and still operate as one-party states, with little formal opposition of any continuing significance. In addition, no guarantee exists that union rank-and-file will reject less than altruistic candidates vying for office. Democratic practices on paper do not translate necessarily into higher standards of ethical conduct, but they may go some of way toward changing underlying culture if critically minded and independent-thinking members become more involved in governance and administration.

A potentially more effective program of remediation, therefore, would go beyond promoting grassroots democracy, which includes protecting the right to dissent. It would encompass transparency in financial reporting and recordkeeping; independent auditing of all aspects of financial affairs; bans on union-leader-sponsored charities, prohibitions on union leaders (current or former) serving on corporate boards for compensation or on the boards of nonprofits like the Union Building Corporation that directed the expenditure of union funds without independent oversight; independent ethics and investigations officers to enforce prohibitions on unethical conduct; and strict financial controls on vendor contracting and expenses charged by union officials and employees. A strong program would further draw a firewall between corporate funds and union operations, limiting the array of activities that might be subsidized to those that focus strictly on representing union members in their relations with management such as in the grievance process (e.g., for example, granting paid time leave to union representatives to perform legitimate labor-management representation activities). Finally, a comprehensive reform program would address the legitimacy of paying the legal fees of union officers who are under investigation, especially when there have been convictions of others implicated in related activities.[44]

Having a multi-pronged approach to ethics reform or stewardship, however, may not be sufficient to ward off any future misconduct, even if accompanied by democratic protections. While the UAW's history shows a strong commitment to ethics, leading to its landmark Ethical Practices Codes in 1957 and the subsequent adoption of a Public Review Board (PRB), its good intentions proved inadequate to deter the current scandal. In the not too distant past, Ewing spoke to the presumptive adequacy of the union's then-extant ethical standards:

As corporate executives, citizens, and policymakers wrestle with a succession of scandals in the business world, what lessons might be drawn from the UAW's experience? Increasingly, the direction of public policy in business ethics is to require increased transparency; that, for example, is the thrust of much of Sarbanes-Oxley. The UAW's experience would imply that this is not enough. Financial malfeasance can be proscribed, conflicts of interest identified and regulated, and more disclosure required in an attempt to increase transparency. Violations can be prosecuted and legal penalties imposed. However, effective enforcement, the kind that creates a truly ethical culture, depends heavily on the existence of democratic procedures to give shareholders (as well as more broadly defined stakeholders) the means to hold institutions accountable.[45]

Perhaps the biggest threats to the practice and maintenance of ethical conduct in unions (or any other association for that matter) include complacency, laxity, and temptation. There is no simple means of preventing these flaws from taking hold. But transparency, independent oversight, and the protection of the right to dissent and criticize offer tools to combat these tendencies.

Does the Current Situation at the UAW Merit a Government Takeover?

Considerable discussion has occupied space in the media about the question of whether the federal government should take over the UAW. The takeover of the IBT, which lasted for approximately three decades, may point in this direction. However, we believe that the situations involving the UAW and IBT are distinctly different. First, and most important, the IBT was heavily infiltrated by organized crime at all organizational levels and across a number of locals. The criminal activity at the UAW, on the other hand, has involved comparatively few individuals and been confined to a limited range of activities. At its worse, it involved clusters of a small number of leaders affiliated the International, Region 5, the UAW-Chrysler NTC, and the UAW-GM CHR. Only a handful of corporate officials associated with the NTC had direct involvement. Though the efforts to corrupt the collective bargaining process and the associated financial subsidization of the UAW through the training centers raise cognate concerns, and certainly may smack in some instances of racketeering, they did not connote the presence of organized crime as conventionally interpreted.

Second, and relatedly, outside of these pockets of wrongdoing, no hard evidence of wider corruption has surfaced (though GM's amended civil RICO suit raises this possibility). At the IBT, federal investigators and prosecutors pursued cases against hundreds of union officials. The sheer volume of corruption in the IBT relative to the UAW appears to distinguish the Teamsters' situation by orders of magnitude.

Third, a government takeover, based on the IBT experience, comes at a heavy financial price. The taxpayers had to bear considerable costs and the union itself had to divert a lot of money toward compliance. This is money, from hardworking dues-payers, that does not go to representing them to secure better contracts, at least in a direct sense. At the very least, any government takeover should be adjusted to the nature and scope of wrongdoing involved, with a strategy for a timely exit.

Last, reforms in financial and democratic practices in and of themselves do not guarantee ethical conduct. Nor do they necessarily prevent organizational bureaucracies from taking on a life of their own and inculcating a culture of corruption.

Perhaps the best remedy for the UAW at this time would be a well-planned constitutional convention that involved a discussion of these challenges and longer-term review of its administration and governance. The union might benefit greatly from changing its staffing and personnel policies and practices to create a more inclusive and tolerant culture of dissent and differing points of view.

Notes

1 Lawrence, 2020, January 24, *op. cit.*; Lawrence, E.D. (2020, June 23). UAW Activitists Say They Should be Able to Attend Gamble's Meeting with US Attorney, *Detroit Free Press.*
2 Jacobs and Cooperman, *op. cit.*
3 Estey et al., *op. cit.*
4 Stieber, *op. cit.*
5 Ibid.
6 Jacobs and Cooperman, *op. cit.*
7 GM Civil RICO Complaint, *op. cit.*; GM Amended Civil Complaint, *op. cit.*
8 Ibid.; Mickens, Plea Bargain, *op. cit.*
9 Burden and Snell, *op. cit.*
10 Iacobelli, Indictment, *op. cit.*
11 Baldas, T., and Lawrence, E. (2017, July 26). Feds: UAW, FCA Execs Were in Cahoots in Multimillion-Dollar Scam that funded trips, cars, *Detroit Free Press.*
12 UAW (2017, July 26). Letter regarding DOJ Investigation. *UAW News Release.*
13 Baldas & Lawrence, *op. cit.*
14 UAW News Release, July 26, 2017, *op. cit.*; Wall-Howard, P. (2019, March 13). UAW President vows to put carmakers on the defensive in contract talks. *Detroit Free Press*; UAW News Release (2019, November 13). United Auto Workers Acting President Rory Gamble enacts immediate nationwide ethics reforms.
15 Howes and Snell, *op. cit.*
16 Ibid.
17 Ibid.
18 Ibid.
19 UAW News Release (2020, March 31). UAW Implements Ethics Reform Priorities with Hiring of First-Ever Ethics Officer and Activation of Confidential Ethics Hotline.

20 Hall, K., Snell, R., and Noble, B. (2019, November 21). Gary Jones Resigns as UAW president, As Union Moved to Expel Him, *Detroit News*.
21 UAW News Release (2020, January 31). UAW Executive Board Files Article 31 Charges to Expel Former Officers and Staff Who Have Been Convicted of Criminal and Unethical Conduct.
22 Ibid.
23 Ibid.
24 UAW News Release (2019, December 5). UAW International Executive Board Appoints Rory Gamble President.
25 UAW News Release (2019, December 6). UAW International Executive Board Announces Region 5 Will Be Merged.
26 Lawrence, 2020, January 24, *op. cit.*
27 Lawrence, 2020, June 23, *op. cit.*.
28 Jacobs, *op. cit.*; Jacobs and Cooperman, *op. cit.*
29 Ibid.
30 Ibid.; Estey et. al., *op. cit.*
31 Ibid.
32 Ibid.
33 Jacobs and Cooperman, *op. cit.*
34 Ibid.
35 Ibid.
36 Ibid.
37 Ibid.
38 Ibid.
39 Ibid.
40 Ibid.
41 Ibid.
42 Jacobs and Cooperman, *op. cit.*, p. 222.
43 Ibid.
44 The UAW allows for the payment of the legal fees of officers who may be under investigation for wrongdoing under limited circumstances which raise doubt about the legitimacy of the inquiry. In its 2019 LM-2 financial disclosure report the UAW revealed that it paid for the legal fees for five current or former officers, including Dennis Williams ($320,912) and Gary Jones ($24,599).
45 Ewing, *op. cit*, p. 266.

Epilogue

Since we finished writing this book, major developments have wreaked economic havoc and provoked widespread social unrest in the United States and worldwide. The COVID-19 pandemic, which began its rapid spread in the US in March 2020, forced the nation to shutdown non-essential activities, including auto manufacturing. Most civilian activities, including court proceedings, were interrupted, unless life or property were threatened. While the nation across the 50 states has begun to reopen the economy, the return has been uneven and choppy. Through this pandemic, organizations of all non-essential types, including unions like the UAW, had their operations disrupted as they moved rapidly into a virtual mode. The national shutdown threw the US economy into a tailspin, from which it has only recently begun to recover. This downturn has implications for the longer-term well-being of auto manufacturing. And just as the US began to relax the lockdowns, it witnessed the tragic killing of George Floyd at the hands of Minneapolis police officers, which triggered waves of demonstrations addressing the nation's vexing struggle with racial injustice. These events singularly and in combination forced any news about the UAW scandal into the background.

On December 14, 2020, the UAW and the U.S. Attorney's office announced a settlement of the investigation of the scandal at the UAW. The terms, which require approval of a federal district judge, include the appointment of an independent monitor for six years and that members be given the option to determine how to elect its international officers going forward. The union faces continuing investigations of the scandal by the US Attorney, the possibility of a government takeover, defendants awaiting sentence, and a dissident faction seeking reform. The UAW, parenthetically, is operating under the hardship brought about by a massive fire that destroyed much of Solidarity House in July 2019, forcing the union to establish temporary headquarters at a different location in the metropolitan Detroit area.

More specifically, on June 3, 2020, former International President Gary Jones pled guilty to embezzlement and racketeering. Given that Jones had cooperated with federal prosecutors, he received an indication of a potentially more lenient sentence. According to a report in the *Detroit News*, Jones implicated his predecessor, Dennis Williams, in a pattern of wrongdoing, which included using UAW and training center funds to refurbish living facilities at Black Lake, building a new cottage for himself at the same location, and partaking in the high-life that a close-knit group of UAW leaders engineered through embezzlement:

> Retired United Auto Workers President Dennis Williams helped embezzle more than $1 million spent on personal luxuries and illegally used money from Detroit automakers to renovate the union's northern Michigan resort, where the union built him a $1.3 million lakefront home, according to federal court records. The allegations are outlined in the 45-page deal his successor, former President Gary Jones, reached with prosecutors to plead guilty Wednesday to embezzlement, racketeering and tax charges. The deal provides the first glimpse into cooperation from Jones in exchange for a shorter prison sentence and reveals two longtime friends and union allies pitted against each other during the federal probe.[1]

It has since been reported that the UAW has accepted an offer to buy Cabin #4, the new plush cottage built for Williams at Black Lake, pending the release of a lien on the property by federal prosecutors.[2]

Facing continuing investigations by the US Attorney, the UAW's International President Rory Gamble and US Attorney Matthew Schneider agreed to discuss the steps necessary to rid the UAW of corruption. A press release issued by the UAW (June 15, 2020) stated that:

> US Attorney Matthew Schneider and UAW President Rory L. Gamble jointly announce that they will be meeting on June 30, 2020 in Detroit in order to begin negotiations to further the cause of reform in the United Auto Workers Union. Both men seek to work together to restore the trust and confidence of the UAW's membership in the Union's ability to represent them and their interests. This meeting is the first step in a joint effort by US Attorney Schneider and President Gamble to put into place mechanisms and protections to eliminate corruption and to ensure that it does not return. US Attorney Schneider commended President Gamble's efforts towards reform and his willingness to take further efforts to combat corruption.[3]

A dissident group affiliated with UAWD had requested to participate in this forthcoming meeting, though the US Attorney rejected the request:

> A group of activists pushing for change at the UAW said it should also be allowed to take part when US Attorney Matthew Schneider meets

with Rory Gamble, the union's president, on June 30. That won't be happening, according to Schneider's office. Spokeswoman Gina Balaya said the meeting will only include representatives of the US Attorney's Office and executives of the UAW. But the group, Unite All Workers for Democracy, said reforms Gamble has instituted since he was elevated to the union's presidency last year do not adequately involve input from the union's membership.[4]

The US Attorney and President Gamble met on June 30, 2020 to discuss the reforms that had been instituted by union as well as other measure that might be undertaken. Lawrence reported that "Both sides agreed a number of reform options 'are on the table and that will be the subject of further negotiations when the parties meet again to consider them in further detail within the coming weeks,' according to a joint news release following the afternoon meeting in Detroit."[5] This represents a positive step toward reaching an amicable solution to reform question that could hopefully avoid a government takeover.

As noted, on December 14, 2020, the UAW and U.S. Attorney Schneider announced a settlement, which ended the investigation into misconduct at the UAW. The parties' settlement, which requires approval of a federal judge, provides for an independent monitor to supervise elections, among other things, for six years. The settlement also grants members the opportunity to determine how they want to elect international officers. In the process of negotiating this settlement, the UAW had repaid the joint training centers for questionable chargebacks and also reimbursed the IRS for relevant "administrative fees" (https://www.freep.com/story/money/cars/2020/12/14/feds-uaw-union-reform-settlement/6542358002/).

As a further update, the US Attorney filed a Criminal Information (Case 2:20-cr-20382-LJM-EAS ECF No. 1 filed 08/27/20) complaint against Dennis Williams, the former UAW International president, for embezzlement on August 27, 2020. According to a report from The Detroit News, this complaint may be a prelude to a guilty plea by the former president.[6] The US Attorney indicated that the investigation at the UAW was continuing but that this latest development was an important step.

Notes

1 Snell, R., Noble, B., and Hall, K. (2020, June 4). Former UAW President Pleads Guilty to Helping Steal More Than $1 Million. *The Detroit News*.
2 Snell, R., and Howes, D. (2020, June 10). UAW Accepts Offer on Controversial Black Lake Home Built for Dennis Williams. *The Detroit News*.
3 United Auto Workers News Release (2020, June 15). US Attorney Matthew Schneider and UAW President Rory L. Gamble Set Meeting for Negotiations Over Reform of the UAW.
4 Lawrence, 2020, June 23, *op. cit.*

5 Lawrence, E.D. (2020, July 1). UAW President, US Attorney Meet on Reforms, Independent Monitor, Election Changes Possible. *Detroit Free Press*.
6 https://www.detroitnews.com/story/business/autos/2020/08/27/ex-uaw-boss-ex-uaw-boss-williams-charged-in-racketeering-scand-williams-charged-racketeering-scandal/5642204002/

Bibliography

Adams, T. (2010). *UAW Incorporated: The Triumph of Capital*. PhD Dissertation, Michigan State University.

Adams, T. (2019, August 19). A Tale of Corruption by the United Auto Workers and the Big Three American Manufacturers, *MR Online*.

Automotive News (2019). The UAW-Detroit 3 2019 Negotiations. Retrieved July 15, 2020. https://www.autonews.com/assets/html/uaw2019/index.html.

Baime, A.J. (2014). *The Arsenal of Democracy: FDR, Detroit, and an Epic Quest to Arm an America at War*. Boston: Houghton Mifflin Harcourt.

Baldas, T., and Lawrence, E. (2017, July 26). Feds: UAW, FCA Execs Were in Cahoots in Multimillion-Dollar Scam that Funded Trips, Cars. *Detroit Free Press*.

Barnard, J. (2004). *American Vanguard: The United Auto Workers during the Reuther Years, 1935–1970*. Detroit: Wayne State University Press.

Bickley, J. M. (2008). *Chrysler Corporation Loan Guarantee Act of 1979: Background, Provisions, and Cost*. Congressional Research Service, RL40005, December 17.

Brooks, C. (2020, March). The Death and Life of the United Auto Workers. *In These Times*, 24–31.

Burden, M. and Snell, R. (2017, July 26). Former FCA Exec, Wife of Former UAW VP Indicted. *The Detroit News*.

Cannis, B., Bickley, J.M., Chaikind, H., Pettit, C.A., Purcell, P., Rapaport, C., and Shorter, G. (2009). *US Motor Vehicle Industry: Federal Assistance and Restructuring*. Congressional Research Service. R40003, May 29.

Cannis, B. and Yacobucci, B.D. (2010). *The US Motor Vehicle Industry: Confronting a New Dynamic in the Global Economy*. Congressional Research Service. R41154, March 26.

Congressional Research Service (2018) *The State of Campaign Finance Policy: Recent Developments and Issues for Congress*, R41542, December 13.

Cooney, S. (2007). *Motor Vehicle Manufacturing Employment: National and State Trends and Issues*. Congressional Research Service, RL34297.

Cutcher-Gershenfeld, J., Brooks, D., and Mulloy. M. (2015). *Inside the Ford-UAW Transformation: Pivotal Events in Valuing Work and Delivering Results*. Cambridge, MA: MIT Press.

Dixon, J. (2001, May 18). A Shroud of Secrecy Surrounds Joint Funds. *The Detroit News*.

Dziczek, K., Chen, Y., and Schultz, M. (2020). *Contribution of General Motors to the Economies of Nine States and the United States in 2019*. Ann Arbor, MI: Center for Automotive Research.

Dziczek, K. (2015, June 23). *Attracting, Developing & Retaining Automotive Talent in Michigan*. Center for Automotive Research Industry Briefing.

Dziczek, K. (2015, June 23). *What's Ahead for 2015 UAW Negotiations with FCA*. Center for Automotive Research Industry Briefing.

Estey, M.S., Taft, P., and Wagner, M. (eds.) (1964). *Regulating Union Government*. New York: Harper & Row Publishers.

Ewing, L. (2005). Ethical Practices in a Labor Union: The Case of the UAW, in J. Budd and J. Scoville (Eds.), *The Ethics of Human Resources and Industrial Relations*. Champaign, IL: Labor and Employment Relations Association.

Ford Motor Company (2015). *2015 UAW-Ford: National Negotiations Media Fact Book*.

Ford Motor Company (2019). *2019 UAW-Ford: National Negotiations Media Fact Book. 2015 UAW-Ford: National Negotiations Media Fact Book*.

Freeman, R.B. and Medoff, J. (1984). *What Do Unions Do?* New York: Basic Books.

Goeddeke, F., and Masters, M.F. (2020). The United Auto Workers: From Walter Reuther to Rory Gamble, *Perspectives At Work*, forthcoming.

Greenhouse, S. (2019). *Beaten Down, Worked Up: The Past, Present, and Future of American Labor*. New York: Alfred A. Knopf.

Hall, K., Snell, R., and Noble, B. (2019, November 21). Gary Jones Resigns as UAW President, As Union Moved to Expel Him. *Detroit News*.

Hart, W.R. (1961). *Collective Bargaining in the Federal Civil Service*. New York: Harper & Brothers Publishers.

Hill, K. and Maranger-Menk, D. (2015, January). *Contribution of the Automobile Industry to the Economies of All Fifty States and the United States*. Ann Arbor, MI: Center for Automotive Research.

Hirsch, B.T. and MacPherson, D.A. (2003). Union Membership and Coverage Database from the Current Population Survey: Note. *Industrial and Labor Relations Review*, 56(2), 349–354.

Howes, D. (2019, September 4). Probe Looms Over UAW-GM Talks. *The Detroit News*.

Howes, D. and Snell, R. (2019, December 18). Driven by Greed: Alliance of FCA, Union Leaders Fueled Decade of Corruption. *The Detroit News*.

Hyde, P. (2004). *Position Paper Outline: UAW Joint Funds Are Not a "Labor-management Committee" Under 29 USC 186(c)(9) But Are, Rather, Labor Trusts Mandated to Make Audits Available for Inspection Pursuant to 29u.S.C. § 186(c)(5)(B)*, Policy and Law Adviser, Office of Labor-Management Standards, US Department of Labor, Presented to the Office of the Solicitor General.

Jacobs, J.B. (2006). *Mobsters, Unions, and the Feds: The Mafia and the American Labor Movement*. New York: New York University Press.

Jacobs, J.B. and Cooperman, K.T. (2011). *Breaking the Devil's Pact: The Battle to Free the Teamsters from the Mob*. New York: New York University Press.

Katz, H.C., MacDuffie, J.P., and Pil, F.K. (2013). Crisis and Recovery in the US Auto Industry: Tumultuous Times for a Collective Bargaining Pacesetter, in H.R. Stanger, P.F. Clark, and A.C. Frost (Eds.) *Collective Bargaining Under Distress:*

Case Studies of North American Industries. Champaign, IL: Labor and Employment Relations Association, pp. 45–80.

Krisher, T., and White, E. (2020, June 11). UAW Accepts Offer on Up North Lake Home Built for Ex-President. *Detroit Free Press.*

Lafer, G. (2017). *The One-Percent Solution: How Corporations Are Remaking America One State at a Time.* Ithaca, NY: ILR Cornell University Press.

Lawrence, E.D. (2020, January 24). UAW Reformers Want to Change How Leaders Are Picked. *Detroit Free Press.*

Lawrence, E.D. (2020, June 23). UAW Activists Say They Should be Able to Attend Gamble's Meeting with US Attorney. *Detroit Free Press.*

Lawrence, E.D. (2020, July 1). UAW President, US Attorney Meet on Reforms, Independent Monitor, Election Changes Possible. *Detroit Free Press.*

Lawrence, E. D. (2020, August 3). GM: Millions of Dollars in Offshore Bank Accounts Fueled Fiat Chrysler Scheme. *Detroit Free Press.*

Lawrence, E. (2020, August 17). GM Presses Ahead with Appeal in Racketeering Suit Against Fiat Chrysler. *Detroit Free Press.*

Lawrence, E.D. (2019, January 5). Up North UAW Resort Bleeds Millions, Plans Controversial Lavish Cabin. *Detroit Free Press.*

Lawrence, E.D. and LaReau, J. (2020, July 8). Judge Dismisses GM Racketeering Suit Against FCA. *Detroit Free Press.*

Lawrence, E. and Wisely, J. (2020, March 5). Ex-UAW President Gary Jones Charged in Corruption Probe. *Detroit Free Press.*

Levitan, S.A. and Loewenberg, J.J. (1964). The Politics and Provisions of the Landrum-Griffin Act, in Estey*et al., op. cit.*, pp. 28–64.

Lipset, S.M., Trow, M., and Coleman, J. (1956). *Union Democracy: What Makes Democracy Work in Labor Unions and Other Organizations.* New York: Anchor Books.

Lutz, H. (2019, November 25). GM Goes to War Against FCA. *Automotive News.*

Lutz, H. (2020, June 17). Court Sets Aside Portion of GM Suit vs. FCA. *Automotive News.*

Masters, M.F. (1997). *Unions at the Crossroads: Strategic Membership, Financial, and Political Perspectives.* Westport, CT: Quorum Books.

Mayer, G. (2004, August 31). *Union Membership Trends in the United States.* Congressional Research Service Report, RL 32252.

McAlinden, S. (2015, June 23). *Some Mild Commentary and Observations Regarding D3-UAW Bargaining for a New Labor Agreement.* Detroit, MI: Center for Automotive Industry Briefing.

McAldinden, S., Dziczek, K., and Schwartz, A. (2011, November 29). *2011 Detroit 3–UAW Labor Contract Negotiations.* Michigan: Center for Automotive Research Breakfast Briefing Schoolcraft Community College Livonia.

McAlinden, S.P. and Chen, Y. (2012, December). *After the Bailout: Future Prospects for the US Auto Industry.* Ann Arbor, MI: Center for Automotive Research.

Noble, B. (2020, June 22). UAW Training Center Reforms Seek Transparency, Higher Standards. *The Detroit News.*

Office of Labor Management Standards (2019, January). *2018 Annual Report.* https://www.dol.gov/agencies/olms/about/annual-reports/2018

Rattner, S. (2010). *Overhaul: An Insider's Account of the Obama Administration's Emergency Rescue of the Auto Industry.* Boston: Houghton Mifflin Harcourt.

Reuther, V.G. (1976). *The Brothers Reuther and the Story of the UAW/A Memoir.* Boston: Houghton Mifflin Company.

Rosenfeld, J. (2014). *What Unions No Longer Do.* Cambridge, MA: Harvard University Press.

Schwartz, A.R. (2015, June 23). *Leading Up to the 2015 UAW-Detroit Three Talks.* Center for Automotive Research Conference. https://www.cargroup.org/wp-content/uploads/2017/02/IB_Jun2015_art_shwartz.pdf.

Seidman, J. (1964). Emergence of Concern with Union Government and Administration, in Estey*et al., op. cit.,* pp. 1–27.

Serrin, W. (1973). *The Company and the Union: The "Civilized" Relationship between General Motors and the United Automobile Workers.* New York: Alfred A. Knopf.

Shermer, E.T. (2008). Origins of the Conservative Ascendancy: Barry Goldwater's Early Senate Career and the De-legitimization of Organized Labor. *Journal of American History,* 94 (December): 678–709.

Snell, R. (2019, October 8). Feds Probe Whether Detroit Carmakers Helped Fund Dennis Williams' UAW Cabin. *The Detroit News.*

Snell, R. (2020, August 14). Judge Refuses to Revive GM Racketeering Suit v. FCA. *The Detroit News.*

Snell, R., and Howes, D. (2020, June 10). UAW Accepts Offer on Controversial Black Lake Home Built for Dennis Williams. *The Detroit News.*

Snell, R., Noble, B., and Hall, K. (2020, June 4). Former UAW President Pleads Guilty to Helping Steal More Than $1 Million. *The Detroit News.*

Snell, R., Noble, B., and Howes, D. (2020, March 5). Former UAW President Gary Jones in Embezzlement Scheme. *The Detroit News.*

Spero, S.D. (1948). *Government as Employer.* Carbondale, IL: Southern Illinois University Press.

Stein, E. (1964). Union Finance and LMRDA, in Estey*et al., op. cit.,* pp. 130–153.

Stieber, J. (1962). *Governing the UAW.* New York: John Wiley and Sons, Inc.

Thibodeau, I., and Howes, D. (2019, December 6). UAW Moving to Disband Region 5 Embroiled in Federal Probe. *Detroit Free Press.*

UAW News Release (2020, January 31). UAW Executive Board Files Article 31 Charges to Expel Former Officers and Staff Who Have Been Convicted of Criminal and Unethical Conduct.

UAW News Release (2020, March 31). UAW Implements Ethics Reform Priorities with Hiring of First-Ever Ethics Officer and Activation of Confidential Ethics Hotline.

UAW News Release (2020, June 15). US Attorney Matthew Schneider and UAW President Rory L. Gamble Set Meeting for Negotiations Over Reform of the UAW.

UAW News Release (2019, November 13). United Auto Workers Acting President Rory Gamble Enacts Immediate Nationwide Ethics Reforms.

UAW News Release (2019, December 5). UAW International Executive Board Appoints Rory Gamble President.

UAW News Release (2019, December 6). UAW International Executive Board Announces Region 5 Will Be Merged.

UAW News Release (2017, July 26). Letter regarding DOJ Investigation.

United Auto Workers (2020). 2019 Contracts with Hourly Employees for FCA, Ford, and GM.

United Auto Workers (2020). *Constitution of the International Union.* https://uaw.org/uaw-constitution-2/.

United Auto Workers (2020, March 5). UAW Statement on Court Filing of Former UAW Member Gary Jones.

US Attorney's Office, Eastern District of Michigan (2020, June 3). Former UAW President Gary Jones Pleads Guilty to Embezzlement, Racketeering, and Tax Evasion. Press Release.

Wall-Howard, P. (2019, March 13). UAW President Vows to Put Carmakers on the Defensive in Contract Talks. *Detroit Free Press.*

Wall-Howard, P. (2020, July 15). FCA to Change Its Name to Stellantis After Merger with PSA in 2021. *Detroit Free Press.*

Wolfcale, J. (2015, June 10). Sergio Marchionne Wants to Merge with General Motors. *Topspeed.*

Legal (Criminal And Civil) Complaints and Plea Bargains

https://nilrr.org/2020/06/15/view-the-plea-deals-behind-the-uaw-corruption-headlines/

Selected Criminal Complaints, Sentencing Memoranda, and Plea Agreements

All sources are from the US Attorney's Office in Eastern District of Michigan, Matthew Schnieder, US Attorney.*General Motors LLC v. FCA US LLC* (E.D. Mich. June 23, 2020) Case No. 19-cv-13429.

US Sixth Circuit Court of Appeals, *General Motors LLC v. FCA US LLC,* July 6, 2020, No. 20-1616.

General Motors LLC v. FCA US LLC (E.D. Mich. July 8, 2020) Case No. 19-cv-13429.

United States of America v. Dennis Williams, Plea Agreement, Case No. 2:20-cr-20382, US District Court, Eastern District of Michigan, September 30, 2020.

United States of America v. Dennis Williams, Criminal Information, Case No. 2:20-cr-20382, US District Court, Eastern District of Michigan, August 27, 2020.

United States of America v. Gary Jones, Plea Agreement, Case No. 2:19-cr-20726, US District Court, Eastern District of Michigan, June 3, 2020.

United States of America v. Alphons Iacobelli & Monica Morgan, Indictment, Case No. 2:17-cr-20406, US District Court, Eastern District of Michigan, July 26, 2017.

United States of America v. Norwood Jewell, Plea Agreement, Case No. 2:19-cr-20146, US District Court, Eastern District of Michigan, April 2, 2019.

United States of America v. Joseph Ashton, Plea Agreement, Case No. 2:19-cr-20738, US District Court, Eastern District of Michigan, December 5, 2019.

United States of America v. Michael Grimes, Plea Agreement, Case No. 2:19-cr-20520, US District Court, Eastern District of Michigan, September 4, 2019.

United States of America v. Jeffery Pietrzyk, Plea Agreement, Case No. 2:19-cr-20630, US District Court, Eastern District of Michigan, October 22, 2019.

United States of America v. Eugene N. Robinson, Plea Agreement, Case No. 2:19-cr-20726, US District Court, Eastern District of Michigan, March 2, 2020.

United States of America v. Vance Pearson, Plea Agreement, Case No. 2:19-cr-20726, US District Court, Eastern District of Michigan, February 2, 2020.

United States of America v. Jerome Durden, Plea Agreement, Case No. 2:17-cr-20406, US District Court, Eastern District of Michigan, August 8, 2017.

United States of America v. Keith Mickens, Plea Agreement, Case No. 2:17-cr-20406, US District Court, Eastern District of Michigan, April 5, 2018.

United States of America v. Michael Brown, Plea Agreement, Case No. 2:17-cr-20406, US District Court, Eastern District of Michigan, May 25, 2018.

United States of America v. Virdell King, Plea Agreement, Case No. 2:17-cr-20406, US District Court, Eastern District of Michigan, August 29, 2017.

United States of America v. Nancy A. Johnson, Plea Agreement, Case No. 2:17-cr-20406, US District Court, Eastern District of Michigan, July 23, 2018.

Index

Printed in the United States
by Baker & Taylor Publisher Services